For Betty —
Happiness always
Nickie McWhirter

Pea Soup

The Best of

Nickie McWhirter

Detroit Free Press

Published by the Detroit Free Press

321 W. Lafayette Blvd.

Detroit, Michigan 48231

Pea Soup
The Best of Nickie McWhirter
Editing: Pat Dunphy
Design: Milt Kelsey
Keyboarding: Barbara Farnham
Co-ordinator: Bill Diem

Manufactured in the United States of America.

ISBN 0-9605692-5-1

Introduction

A formal introduction in a book is as rare today as a formal introduction in a fern bar, and for some of the same reasons.

We have become an impatient society, eager to get to the main course and skip the appetizers. We are eager to enjoy our pleasures and rewards without satisfying protocols. We have largely given up on deferred gratification.

Not long ago, deferred gratification was the accepted and most acceptable way of American life.

Be patient, my son. Prepare yourself diligently and, with hard work, you may become president of the United States, or foreman of the paint and trim department at the Chrysler Jefferson Avenue plant.

Be patient, my daughter. Someday your Prince will find you, love you at first sight and whisk you off to his palace (with a view from every parapet) where you will live happily ever after.

Meanwhile, boys and girls, study hard in school, mind your manners, guard your chastity, go to church on Sunday, salute the flag and always mind your parents. The future is yours! But not immediately, you understand.

Then came the revolution.

It began with cataclysmic explosions in the decade of the 1960s. The nation was at war in Vietnam, embarrassed and confused to be so, ashamed and outraged at its own shame.

The civil rights movement had come of age and was marching through Washington, D.C., and backroads in Mississippi with politicians on either arm. Business leaders were perplexed; some were outraged. There was this ominous-sounding new idea called affirmative action which was about to shatter long-existing hiring, firing, pay and promotion practices.

Teenagers were leaving home, letting their hair grow, turning on to drugs, dropping out of schools, preaching universal love and peace at the same time they splashed hatred and violence in all directions at once.

The pill was acclaimed the liberator of women. It made possible, for women and their men, casual sex, open marriage and assorted loving experiments other than legal, monogamous marriage, without fear of unwanted pregnancies. Feminism was in bud and soon burst into savage bloom.

The revolution was on all fronts and touched every one of us. There was no escape, not in age or geography, theology or philosophy. It changed everyone, even loyalist resisters. At the very least, it demanded that each of us re-examine our cherished values and our long-held views of propriety and try to survive in a culture newly re-designed in a seemingly helter-skelter fashion.

This book is about that challenge, which continues.

It comprises a collection of newspaper columns written from 1977 to the present, a selection from more than 1,000 such snippets which appeared originally in the Detroit Free Press and, through syndication, in other newspapers throughout the United States and Canada.

Their common subject is loving, coping, living — well and not so well — in a post-revolutionary culture, much altered from what it was only yesterday.

A word about the title is in order.

A friend suggested this collection be titled, "Nickie McWhirter . . . Her Secret Shame: She Finks on Her Friends!" I thought that accurate, but harsh. I also rejected calling the book "Fred" — the suggestion of one weary senior editor after a long afternoon.

I chose "Pea Soup," which is a metaphor for the human condition. The selection which follows explains everything you could possibly want to know about all this — I think.

— *Nickie McWhirter*

Life's a kettle of pea soup, and there's no escaping it

One thing that happens when you start writing a newspaper column is that old friends and acquaintances you haven't thought about in years send you friendly letters and invite you to lunch. Everybody wants to find out what's happened in your life since last you met. They also want to tell you what's happened in theirs. This can be boring, or fascinating, depending on the folks.

I knew this brainy, intense young woman, for example, who was just out of college about 20 years ago when I, too, was a tadpole. I quit a job at McGraw-Hill Publishing Co. and she took over my chores. I figured I would go home and have three babies in three minutes, which I did, and then live happily ever after as housewife and mother, which I did not.

I figured she would probably hang in for 30 years or so of ladder-climbing and then take over as managing editor of the New York Times. She seemed that committed to corporate politics and the paste pots.

I got a letter from her last week. She's a librarian in Grand Rapids.

This is a good example of what happens to people caught up in the General Chaos.

I have this General Chaos Theory, you see, which explains a great deal of the unpredictability, aggravation and misery, as well as the good fortune which manifests itself in human lives. It's a very complex theory, developed over many years, but I will share some of it with you.

We are all plunked into the General Chaos at birth. Think of it as pea soup. People are the lumps. There is no escape.

We are all swirling around in this enormous caldron which contains, in addition to ourselves, all the good and bad things that can possibly affect us. Everything is in there and everything is constantly moving, changing and coming into new alignment.

What happens is that just when we get ourselves fairly well adjusted to our surroundings in our part of this mire and things begin to slow down and settle in — slurp! Somebody stirs the soup.

People who were on the bottom come to the top, and the other way around. What was desirable and within reach disappears. Or, more happily, what was threatening vanishes and what was lovely, but out of reach, bobs up right there, over your left shoulder.

Once you understand the General Chaos Theory, you won't get ulcers — or a big head either. It is definitely irrational to be either desperate or smug in the midst of the General Chaos.

In various of my lectures on this little-understood subject, persons have asked if, under the circumstances, it makes any sense to plan for the future or strive for any short- or long-term goals. Certainly, is the answer.

What you do is plan like blazes and move as quickly as possible. If you want something, you have a much better chance of snaring it with a plan than without one. And, unfortunately for us scientists and theoreticians, it is impossible to predict just when the wooden spoon of life is going to be thrust into the kettle again.

Sometimes it's a beastly long time between stirs; sometimes not at all. That's part of it. Chaos is unpredictable.

If plans go kafritz, of course, the best response is to lie back and relax. You can't fight the General Chaos. Attempts to do so are doomed. I'll give you one example.

There is a man I know who fancied himself in love with a widow. She shared the fancy. It was a sticky arrangement inasmuch as he was married and she lived in another city. He figured the solution was for him to get a divorce, marry the widow and they would figure out the rest later. He began the process.

The General Chaos took a stir and the widow decided she didn't want any part of his plan, or him. For months this poor yahoo exhausted himself trying to figure out what went wrong. He also attempted to regain his lost love, i.e. the position he previously held in the pot. No luck, naturally. He didn't know anything about the General Chaos, so I explained.

Recently, I am pleased to report, this victim is drifting in the maelstrom, more or less contentedly, waiting for things to settle. At that time he will take a look around to see what has surfaced. That's good sense. Knowledge is power.

— *June 15, 1977*

Pea Soup

Liking poets again
. . . even Hopkins

I do not have cancer this week. More precisely, no evidence of cancer turned up yesterday during the annual punch-and-poke session at Henry Ford Hospital. My doctor and I must now wait another week or two, as is our custom, for the write-in votes to be counted. These are cast by people who run computers and peer into microscopes. If they find no blips in my bones, fluids and viscera, I will get on with the business of welcoming spring.

I am a recovered cancer patient. People like me have a touch of the vapors each year, when it's time for the ol' check-up. It has been been some time now since the enemy and I squared off, and the doctors say they think I won, but nobody can be sure.

I am not going to tell you about my operation, and I hope you won't tell me about yours.

It's what happens in people's minds that's important, not what happens in their bodies. I will tell you what happened before, and after, in mine.

In 1971 I still believed I was going to live to be 95 and die in my bed, painlessly, surrounded by my children, grandchildren and great-grandchildren. We would recite Emily Dickinson poems and finally I would go to sleep, wrinkled but still beautiful.

It was a warm Monday night in August when I began to grow up, and about time. There were by then three children, well into puberty, one husband, a dog, a cat, a big house and the usual concerns.

Ed and I were sitting on the screened porch enjoying a hint of cool breeze. I had not been feeling well, but that night I felt wonderful. I had been hospitalized a week earlier for tests, the second time in a year. The doctors couldn't find much wrong. Those laboratory ballots were out. I had decided I was fine.

Ed mixed martinis, and we talked about the day in our separate sweat shops, and we could smell the night-blooming flowers nearby. The world was a pleasant place until the phone rang.

It was the doctor, at 8 p.m. I knew I was in trouble. I heard Ed say, "I think you should tell her. She'll have questions. She's a big girl." I knew I was in big trouble.

A malignant tumor, a rare and mean one. Surgery, as soon as possible. Wednesday? OK. OK. It was going to be all right.

Nobody cried. Nobody panicked. We ate dinner and said good night to the kids. Ed and I talked until midnight about what and how to tell them, and the grandmothers. There were to be no hysterics. It was going to be all right. We slept.

I went to work the next day and told the people who needed to know that I would be away for awhile for repairs occasioned by cancer. They were supportive. That night the kids cried a little and hugged a lot. They wondered if I would like to go to the State Fair. I like watching the animals. I couldn't work up the spirit, so we all stayed home together. I think we popped corn. We laughed. I packed for my adventure — and I was thinking of it in that way — but my hands shook. I took along my guitar, which I was just learning to play, plus ALL my beauty secrets and three heavy books. It was going to be all right.

Tuesday night in the hospital I was finally alone, and scared, and resentful and about to graduate into the human race.

Fear and self pity take many forms. Mine was anger. I raged. The nurses closed the door and let me pummel the pillows. Who the hell pulled this miserable, rotten, unspeakable trick on me anyway? What crummy string of DNA got out of line; what miserable chromosome didn't do its job; what immune mechanism dared break down in my body, and why can't I do something other than just SUBMIT?

I remembered churchy things and said to hell with it. Poets were my refuge. I remembered Gerard Manley Hopkins' "Windhover" and said to hell with poets too, especially him.

My body had failed me and so had my mind. I was alone and I was helpless. I was going to die all right, and not pleasantly either. It was a bad night, growing up.

The surgery went well and so did the recuperation. There were exotic tests every three months, then every six, now just once a year. With decreasing frequency, then, I remember the terror.

There are flashbacks. Every time I have a sore throat or a bellyache, I find myself tracking it and wondering: Is this one different? How long have I had it? Should I tell the doctor? I am aware and wary.

There is an occasional unexpected jolt. I try to give blood in a Red

Cross drive and am told mine is unacceptable. Ditto for a kidney donor card. Insurance is hard to buy, and when I wonder why, I discovered that 80 percent of the people who have had my tumor are dead within 10 years, with or without treatment. It's important to know. I pull for the 20 percent.

I think of these things now only in the month of March, when I hear the sweet verdict that I am still healthy. I know the doctors should say, "as far as we can tell now," but doctors are also human beings. Some of them.

We learn best and most by comparing things. The experience of war teaches the value of peace. When we have been cold, we understand the pleasure of being warm. Spending one night with the prospect of painful, ugly death at a fairly early age puts a much sweeter face on living.

I don't think the stuff we hear in church about hellfire and brimstone or about heavenly rewards does that job. It doesn't teach us to savor life, here and now. I am lucky for the experience I had, and I don't mind my yearly reminders.

I no longer even daydream about what I will do when I am 97. I plan what I will do today and tomorrow and maybe next year. Anything further ahead in time is subject to cancellation without notice.

Laughter has become important. Hassles are a waste of time. Planting a garden is important if I feel like it; ironing is boring. Telling my children I love them and demanding nothing in return is hard, and very important. Giving someone else pleasure in unexpected ways is fun. Loving is good. Hating makes people sick.

I have stopped trying to change myself to suit others. I have stopped trying to change others. I have stopped being married, and I have stopped going to potluck suppers the second Tuesday of every month. I have stopped all of these things for the same reason.

I have started liking poets again, even Hopkins. They go well with springtime.

March 9, 1977

We see our biggest monsters when we're alone

Once, when I was about eight years old, I came home from school to find our house locked and empty. There was a note pinned to the front door from my mom. It said she had gone somewhere. I have forgotten where. Anyway, it said she expected to be home by the time I got there, but just in case she didn't I was not to worry. She would be along soon. I wasn't worried.

I dumped my school stuff on the front porch and headed for the vacant lot, which was our neighborhood playground. It was going to be fun to play in my school shoes and clothes. It never occurred to me that the rules about not scuffing school shoes and not getting mud on school clothes, especially my new (for Easter) navy coat, might still apply. Kids have their own logic.

It was an unsettled early spring day, breezy and slightly cold. The snow was gone and so was the ice, but the ground was damp and chilly, and on this day, there had been no sun. The sky was gray and getting more so.

Before I had time to do much scuffing or muddying, the wind kicked up and the sky got very dark. Thunder began to rumble. A few big, cold drops of rain carried in the wind spattered on our faces. With the very first well-defined thunderclap, all the kids at the lot scattered and went squealing toward their houses. Me too. I was sure Mom would be there, holding the door open for me.

She wasn't. The house was still dark and locked. The note was still on the door, flapping in the wind.

All my friends had vanished behind the closed doors of their houses all over the block. I stood on my front porch, which was one of those open wooden ones with a railing. There was an old porch swing hung from chains at one end. The sky was getting angry. I watched as lamps were switched on here and there in living rooms across the street.

I don't know why I didn't go knock on one of those doors and ask if I could come inside until my mother got home. Kids just didn't do that in my neighborhood. Besides, I had some sense that I belonged at home, even if I couldn't get inside. I felt the wet wind blow, and I shivered.

The sky was rolling smoke, blacker than any I had ever seen. Lightning split through the clouds, and there was an explosion of thunder. The main event began.

Rain came down in heavy curtains, driven by a strong wind that whipped the tree branches back and forth and made the loose ends of the chains on the porch swing go clank, clank, clank, against themselves.

I was scared. I was also very cold and wet. I put my school papers and books between the front and storm doors of the house. I couldn't put myself there. I looked up and down the street for our car and Mom. There was nothing except howling wind and rain, and a few broken tree branches tumbling around.

There was an old braided rug on the porch which hadn't soaked through. I put it on the porch swing, sat in the middle of it, pulled my legs up Indian fashion and wrapped the rug around myself. I watched the storm.

It was more than just watching, I know now. I experienced this storm. That is entirely different. You become part of whatever you experience, and you can't get away from it. Experiencing the storm was a crucial event in my life, although I don't suppose I knew it while it was going on.

Listening to the clank, clank of the chains, hunched up in the rug and rocking gently in the swing, I could feel cold rain pelting my face and shoulders. The thunder and lightning were cosmic forces, gigantic, potentially lethal and totally unreasonable. They terrified me, especially thunder.

I didn't cry. I don't know why. I was sure I would be hit by lightning. I wanted to run across the street to a neighbor, but it was too late. The lightning would get me as soon as I stepped off my porch. I knew that. I would stay put. Besides, I was keeping warm. I wasn't shivering as much.

When I realized that I was keeping warm, the fear went away. It disappeared almost instantly. I don't know why that happened either.

I began to enjoy the drama of the storm. I imagined myself a chipmunk or a rabbit in the open field behind my school. The swing became a hollow log and the rug was a blanket of dry leaves I had stuffed in there against just such an emergency as this. Lord, I was clever! Smartest chipmunk in the field.

I imagined myself a ship's captain on some square-rigger caught in a typhoon. I had lost most of my crew. Washed overboard, poor devils. I was wrapped in oilskins, lashed to the wheel. The rocking swing now became a foundering ship. The clanking chains were damaged rigging. Never mind, me hearties! We'll not hit the rocks! We'll make safe passage through the narrows!

I felt very strong and capable. Go ahead, lightning. You'll never get me now. Not now or ever!

In the middle of one of these fragmented imaginings, our car and my mother arrived. She puddle-jumped to the porch, calling to me, wondering if I was OK, sputtering about the sudden storm, flooded streets and trouble with wet engine parts. She was sorry she was late. She was glad I had wrapped the rug around me. She wasn't mad at all that my new coat was a rumpled, dirty mess. We went into the house.

The chipmunk had survived the flood. The captain had saved the ship. A little girl was proud to say she no longer feared lightning, thunder or similar terrors of terrestrialism. She was invincible!

I had felt the uncontrolled and fearsome power of Nature, maybe the Universe — what does an eight-year-old know? — striking at my shivering body. There was no escape. My own house had been closed to me. My parents, those wise protectors, had deserted me. So had all my friends. I had been afraid and then, mysteriously, not afraid at all. I had come to terms with the storm, endured it and found strength in myself to prevail, wrapped in an old rag rug.

I think we always meet our biggest monsters and most terrifying demons alone. It happens all our lives. Even if we are surrounded by friends and family, the really scary things have to be met and bested on some empty porch with the wind howling and the rain coming down, with the door locked and no one else able to help.

Once you survive such an ordeal, however, the next one is not nearly so tough or scary. That's what I learned on an old porch swing during an Illinois thunderstorm a couple of springs ago. Funny how education works.

— March 24, 1980

I've given up hating: It's a waste of time and energy

There was a shallow stream which rambled through a gully near Columbia Junior High School in Peoria. We called it a creek. It had a gravel bed, and usually the water was only about ankle deep, except in the holes, and except in early spring when a rainstorm could fill the creek up, maybe, three feet deep with fast-running water. I didn't go there to play when this happened. Sometimes I went to sit on the bank and watch the mud run and imagine the Johnstown Flood or Noah and the Ark. Mostly I went to the creek on sunny days, summer and winter. I was about eight years old.

I didn't know much about turtles then. I found them in this creek in the summer, but I could never find them in winter and I wondered why. It didn't make sense to me that they migrated, like birds, because I knew they would have to swim, or walk, and either way it was impractical for a turtle to plan a long trip. Where they went in winter was a puzzlement.

Almost all of life was a puzzlement to me at the time, and a very exciting one. Turtles, live, free-roaming ones — not the dime store variety — were a new discovery. I don't know why I loved them, but I did.

In summer I took off my shoes and socks and waded around in the creek catching turtles. I got very wet, but it felt good, and my mother didn't care as long as I was in play clothes. I watched the turtles pull in their heads and legs when I picked them up and then slowly, slowly extend these appendages again as I held the beasties very still in my hands. The tiny eyes blinked at me. I felt like a giant. Turtles have the smallest toes and toenails I have ever seen. Perfect, too.

Strangely, I never took a turtle home. I carted home kittens, snakes, frogs, grasshoppers, lightning bugs and various other creatures, with various schemes to keep them as pets. I never took turtles. They belonged in the creek, and the creek belonged to me. That was how I had it figured. I never invited any of my friends to see this private place.

One day, one summer, I kicked off the shoes and socks and went turtle-stalking as usual and found much more than I expected, and more than I could handle.

On some large, flat stones at the water's edge lay three turtles, dead and dying. Their shells had been smashed, as if they had been pounded on the rocks or hurled, with great force, against them. Some of the mystery concealed under those once-perfect, patterned backs oozed out onto the stones, mustard yellow, wet and obscene.

I couldn't move in for a closer look. I couldn't even breathe. I just stood there in the running water staring, until my ankles ached. Then I climbed out of the creek and abandoned it, forever, as it turned out.

I walked along the bank headed toward the street that would lead me home. I felt some sense of loss, not loss of three dead turtles, but loss of this place. There was something here that killed things, and if it could do such damage to turtles, it could damage anything. The perfect place was imperfect after all.

About 50 yards downstream, I came upon three other kids, all older and bigger than I was. They were splashing and laughing in the water. They had a baseball bat, and they were smashing turtles.

How does one describe the sudden awakening in the human soul of hatred? It is pure destructive energy. I still remember those three faces, every freckle and squint. I screamed at them, but they only laughed.

I ran home, but I did not cry. I was consumed with hatred. It is the first and only time I have felt that particular emotion. I won't let it hold sway anymore, because of what it did to me that one time.

I used to dream about those kids. I had nightmares, but I wouldn't tell anyone, not even Mom, what was wrong. I nursed the horror and the grudge. I daydreamed that terrible things would happen to those kids. One would be hit by a truck; another would drown in the river; the one who was swinging the bat would fall out of a tree and smash his skull on the ground and it would crack open, just like the turtles' shells.

When I saw those kids in school, I got cold and stiff just looking at them. I considered them abominations, but I was polite. I just hoped they would be struck dead by lightning right in front of me. I wanted to see it.

My hatred did them not one whit of harm, or good. The only person it affected was me. It made me sick. I was a little girl with nightmares, daydreaming about misery and affliction torturing other kids. That's sick. Hating drained a lot of energy and wasted it.

Hating accomplished nothing of value to anybody, especially me. I guess I am more pragmatist than anything else and have been forever. Somewhere along the line, I gave up hating. I don't know when or why.

I remember hatred, however, and how it felt and what it did to me — not them. Now, when I listen to grown-up people nursing grudges, gossiping about real or imagined affronts, planning mini-revenges against people they call "enemies," I think of turtles. I think of time I wasted hating three kids when I should have been telling them what I knew about turtles, which wasn't much, but a little. I knew enough to love them. Maybe I could have taught them that. Maybe together we could have figured out where turtles go in winter.

—Nov. 29, 1978

Keeping the mind monster at bay isn't just child's play

When I was a small child, monsters lived under my bed at night. During daytime hours, they were not present. I didn't need to look to make sure. I knew their habits.

These monsters were not vague, shadowy presences. They were dark brown, furry creatures, about the size of my mother's largest mixing bowl. They had black eyes and huge mouths full of sharp teeth. Their arms and legs were furless and tentacle-like, ending in grasping claws.

What the monsters wanted was to catch a small child, such as myself, when her foot or hand dangled over the edge of the bed at night, in the dark. If that occurred, one of the monsters would wrap a tentacle around the dangling appendage and drag the child under the bed to be devoured. There was no escape, should it have ever come to this.

Catastrophe could be avoided, however. The monsters couldn't attack anything but arms, legs, hands or feet. I don't know why. I just understood this truth. They couldn't move out from under the bed either, and they were powerless to materialize in the presence of grown-ups or light.

It was only necessary, then, to whine for a night light. That failing, one could get into bed and make sure one's hands and feet were fully covered by the benevolent bedsheets before the light was turned off. It was best to be tucked into bed by an adult, who would then turn the light off on the way out.

If there were no adult to perform this mercy, however, a child could still survive. It was possible to switch the light off oneself, run, jump into bed and pull up the covers — all in the single second it took for the monsters to materialize in the darkness under the bed. I did this on many occasions, with my heart in my throat and my feet flying an inch above the floorboards.

A child's imagination is vivid, but quite orderly, you will note. It conceives its own monsters but empowers them to perform their monstrous acts only according to inflexible rules, well understood and controlled by the child. In this way, a child experiments with fear, even terror, and builds into each experiment his or her own fail-safe escape mechanism. And as the child survives, outwitting the monsters over and over again, he or she gathers courage and confidence from each encounter. Pretty soon imaginary monsters are no longer important learning tools. They evaporate.

I suspect all children experience this phenomenon to a greater or lesser degree. Dealing with imaginary monsters may be part of a normal preparation for doing battle with genuine adult terrors. It's certainly part of building self-esteem.

So, I hope adults dealing with children will respect the monsters a child says are under the bed, or in the closet or lurking at the foot of the basement stairs. If a child says they exist, they exist. If a child says certain rituals must be performed to render the monsters powerless, those rituals must be performed, meticulously. Any adult who ridicules such terrors or pushes a child to break his or her own rules concerning monster management does no service to a child, but complicates the child's proper business of learning to manage fear and win, every time.

The craziest part of all is that the same adults who insist little Leroy's monsters are unreal and his odd exorcism rituals are foolish, go to their own beds and toss half the night wrestling with their own, largely imaginary monsters: The prospect of bankruptcy, the possibility of serious illness, of being unloved, of growing old, of losing the account.

As always, grown-ups could learn from children. Every child knows for sure that mind monsters are real, but can be held at bay. You simply pull the covers up to your chin, put your hands under the pillow and don't dangle your feet over the edge of the bed. Grown-ups pop Valium and drink vodka. That's how much we know.

— Feb. 13, 1983

Orphan Annie wristwatch tells a lot more than time

Now that I've grown my fingernails so they're sticking out a half-inch beyond my fingertips, and I don't have even one of them broken or chipped or starting to rip, and I keep them polished . . . now, finally, nobody cares. It's a relief.

When I was a little kid and bit my nails, everybody cared. Everybody said I should let them grow so they'd be "pretty." Everybody made a big noise about fingernails.

Mother put foul-tasting stuff on them to remind me not to bite, but I washed it off. Father frowned at me over the top of his glasses whenever he saw me biting my nails, but I ignored him. My grandmother, the Tyrant, made me wear little white gloves when we went out together because my nails were "a sight." I chewed on the gloves.

My grandfather finally got to me. He said if I would let all my nails grow so he could put a ruler under them and see that they all measured one-eighth inch, he'd buy me a wristwatch. I thought about it. I bargained for the right to bite just one nail and let the others grow. He said that was no deal. I thought about it some more. I really wanted a wristwatch.

I stopped biting my nails. It was hard. Grandpa measured my fingernails with the ruler everyday and sometimes I asked him to do it twice a day. It took five years for them to grow one-eighth inch. That's how I remember it. Anyway, one day Grandpa measured and said he did believe, by golly, it was time to go wristwatch shopping. I was very excited.

Grandpa and I went downtown together. We wouldn't let anybody else come along. We went to lots of stores and had a chocolate soda afterward.

I got an Orphan Annie watch. I really wanted a Mickey Mouse, but Grandpa thought Mickey Mouse watches were for boys, so I got the Orphan Annie, and that was OK with me, too. Grandpa showed me how to set it and wind it, and he strapped it on my wrist. The strap was tan leather.

We rode home on a streetcar. On the way Grandpa asked me twice what time it was. He checked what my Orphan Annie watch said against what his big, gold, pocket watch said. The second time I told Grandpa what time it was, he shook his watch and put it up to his ear to listen to it tick. Then he said his watch must be running a little slow. He pretended to reset it according to what Orphan Annie said. I knew he was pretending. We both laughed.

So, anyway, I had an Orphan Annie wristwatch with a tan leather strap and everybody, even my schoolteachers, wanted to see it. Everybody told me I had very nice fingernails, too.

That was all a long time ago, and by now I've lost the Orphan Annie watch, which is too bad, because I would still wear it every once in a while if I still had it.

I could probably chew my fingernails off tomorrow and nobody would care. I don't feel like doing that, however, and if I ever did I would probably think about Grandpa and Orphan Annie and wouldn't be able to take the first nibble. But I read in one of those psychology magazines that everything my family did to get me to quit biting my nails was wrong. What my grandfather did was especially wrong.

Putting terrible tasting stuff on kids' fingernails to get them to stop chewing is supposed to confuse a child and make her think her mother has a mean streak. Dad shouldn't have glowered at me because that is supposed to make a kid think she's rotten and worthless. The Tyrant shouldn't have inhibited me by insisting I wear gloves. I could have caught a neurosis from that. Grandpa definitely should not have resorted to a bribe, because bribes encourage kids to become emotional extortionists.

Funny, I don't remember being confused by any of it at the time. I knew who loved me. I really wanted to stop chewing my nails. All I needed was a smart grandpa to make stopping special, and easier. Some kids have all the luck. I'm glad nobody in my family was smart enough to be a shrink.

— Nov. 25, 1981

A little girl's aunt shares surprises and sweet secrets

A pal of mine is pregnant, which means I get to be an aunt. I don't have any real-life brothers or sisters, constant readers will recall. This pal is like a sister, however, which is why I absolutely, positively get to be an aunt. She said so. Yippee!

Not only that, through the miracles of modern medicine this mother-to-be already knows she is going to have a baby girl. So I already know I get to be an aunt to a little girl. It's pretty scary. I am not sure how to do it.

I had an aunt named Adele who was nifty but peculiar. Sometimes when Adele went out to dinner with my parents, she wore flapper dresses, rolled stockings, dangle earrings and rouged her knees. She smoked cigarets with a long holder. She drank Pink Ladies and Sloe Gin Fizzes. She was witty and laughed a lot. I thought she was beautiful and I wanted to be just like her.

When Adele wasn't laughing and flapping, she worked as a librarian in St. Louis, Mo. Then she wore eyeglasses, high collars, long sleeves and a very prim expression. There was no rouge anywhere. She shushed people and explained the Dewey decimal system. She was a nervous, finicky grouch.

My father, Adele's brother, used to joke about her dual personality. Then one day Adele began acting really strange and some doctors examined her, shook their heads and finally said she was a genuine schizophrenic, paranoid type. The joking stopped.

I didn't enjoy Adele's full-blown schizophrenic years. I couldn't see the enemies she saw or hear the voices she heard. It was very confusing. She used to cry a lot and I would hug her, and she would hug me and then I would cry. I felt sorry that she didn't laugh and flap anymore.

I had four other aunts. They were the wives of my two uncles. Duke had one wife. Floyd had three — a redhead, a blond and a brunet — serially. They were all OK, except for the redhead, who didn't like kids. Kids didn't like her, either. I don't think I want to be like any of them.

I will try to be like Adele, except for the schizophrenic part. Adele used to buy me things my parents never thought about buying. There were very grown-up shoes and clothes and real jewelry, for example. She took me to elegant restaurants and ordered escargot and told me they were snails. When I made a face she promised I would like them, and I did. We had secrets.

One of the secrets was nail polish. I wasn't supposed to wear it. Adele bought me a bottle of pink nail polish anyway, plus polish remover, cotton balls and a manicure set in a little leather case. She showed me how to polish my nails and how to unpolish my nails. I kept my stuff in the bottom drawer of Adele's dresser. I could only use it when the Tyrant was out of the house. I felt very glamorous.

When I was mad at my mother or father, I could tell Adele about it, and she listened. She never said I was right or wrong or that my parents were right or wrong. She just listened. She told me all parents could be a drag sometimes. It made me feel better and not so helpless.

She told me about boyfriends she had a long time ago in high school. She described how they looked and moved, what they said and did. She made everything sound very romantic and lovely, like a Clark Gable movie. I think now she made a lot of it up. But my parents never talked about boyfriends and girlfriends at all. Adele's romantic stories were very helpful. I was trying to figure out what to say to boys when we weren't out climbing trees and playing baseball.

An aunt gets to be a grown-up friend to a child. An aunt is someone who makes happy surprises when it isn't even your birthday. She is someone waiting and available to help when your parents can't or won't, or when you just don't feel comfortable asking them. She is cheerful and loving but never pushy. She is a combination big sister and older friend who happens to be part of the family. Being a little girl's aunt is going to be fun. I think I'll leave now and buy some baby clothes.

— Aug. 30, 1981

Great cook she wasn't, but Mom could serve a feast

A discussion of Mother's Day and its celebration was under way during cocktail hour at a private club.

"What we must remember," said the tall gentleman in the club tie, artfully swirling the ice in his scotch-with-a-splash, "is that none of our mothers knows how to cook. That's why it's such a pleasure to take them out to dinner."

"Blasphemy," gasped a sweet young thing to his right.

"True is true," the gentleman said. "We only remember mother's cooking as delicious because we were children when we were obliged to eat it. We were always hungry and quite unsophisticated.

The sweet young thing did. So did I.

Almost every Sunday afternoon Mom's brothers and their wives (when they had wives, which was now and then), Mom's father and Suzie (the widow with whom he kept company following the death of my grandmother) and sometimes a married couple named Watkins (close friends of Mom and Dad) came to our house and stayed for dinner.

I played ball with my uncles in the backyard. I listened and pretended to believe the tall tales my grandfather spun for my amusement. I listened to the business discussions of Dad and Mr. Watkins. And I popped in and out of the kitchen where Suzie, Mrs. Watkins and my aunts, if any, spent most of the afternoon watching Mom cook.

The aromas of dinner in preparation were delicious. Kettles and pots steamed on the stove. A blast of hot air, full of meaty smells, warmed my face as I watched Mom open the oven door over and over again to check the roast. The roast might be anything — beef, lamb, veal, rarely pork, but sometimes chickens stuffed with homemade dressing liberally laced with sage Granddad brought from a farm near his house. I liked that smell best of all.

Ultimately, after the potatoes had been mashed and the peas put in a bowl, after the gravy was made and the roast had been transferred to a platter and put at Dad's place at the head of the table, it was time for dinner. A pineapple upside-down cake, made from Bisquick, sat on the kitchen table, waiting its turn to delight us.

"Come to the table, everybody come to the table now before it all gets cold." That's what Mom called, as she shoved a big pan of rolls in the oven, took off her apron and tossed it on a kitchen chair.

"Say 'rolls' to me in 10 minutes," she told the family gathering at the table. "Otherwise I'll forget and they'll burn." And everybody agreed to say, "rolls," but lots of times everybody forgot until the unmistakable smell of charred bread wafted into the dining room and Mom jumped up and ran to the kitchen to salvage what she could.

After "grace" and a ritual carving of the meat and passing of dishes heavy with the bounty, we feasted. I was always starving, but never near enough death to try Suzie's peculiar appearing corn conserve, about which my grandfather alone raved. The rest of the meal was delicious, especially the pineapple upside-down cake.

I know, and probably knew even then, that the peas were hard and starchy and the roast was dry, gray and tasteless from spending much too much time in the oven. The potatoes had lumps. Ditto the gravy. Salads were drowned in bottled dressings. And, of course, the rolls were burned.

But those Sunday dinners were superb. The food was marinated and simmered in love, the very special ingredient you can't get in any restaurant. I will never remember my mother as anything but a culinary genius.

— *May 8, 1983*

Girls do not swing like rusty gates

I didn't know the significant difference between boys and girls until I was 12 years old. All I knew was the anatomical difference. That had been demonstrated years earlier to half a shocked kindergarten class by an obnoxious little boy who became notorious for dropping his drawers along with his galoshes in the cloak room. That's what we called them — galoshes and cloak room.

The difference that counted in those days between boys and girls had to do with available opportunities. Boys had more, in areas that counted. That's what it took me 12 years to find out, and it happened, traumatically, one Saturday morning in July.

In my neighborhood on McClure Street in Peoria there were only three girls: Beverly Baker, Shirley Mau and me. There were at least a dozen boys, however, and we girls all grew up running with the pack.

Every day after school or on vacation days and weekends, this gang of ragtags gathered in the empty lot about six houses away from where I lived. The lot was our Olympic Stadium.

In winter, we split into teams, made snow forts and had monster snowball fights. We outlawed rocks and ice balls, but face-washing was favored. In spring we made and flew kits, wrestled, dug holes, climbed the oak tree that was the only major vegetation surviving and generally made a lot of noise. In summer there were games of kick-the-can, statue, tag, red rover and anything else we could invent that required little equipment and great amounts of energy. Our games were rough, unending and highly verbal. You're out! Safe! No fair tackling around the neck! Indian grip, Indian grip, here comes Hippo! Ollie, ollie oxen free! We all had to go home when the streetlights went on.

Now, I am not one to brag. Anybody who grew up in that gang, however, should you find one today, would tell you that I more than held my own. I ALWAYS got to play catcher or first base in the ball games, and when it came to picking teams of any kind I got chosen near the start of the pick. That tells you something. No brag; truth.

What happened on my day of enlightenment was this: I slept later than usual. When I woke up, I could tell by the sunlight in my bedroom. I was startled that I hadn't heard Wilmer or Bubby (his name was actually Robert) Davidson, or somebody, yell for me at the front door. That's how it was done, this morning roundup on the way to the lot. Somebody yelled your name outside your front door, or under your bedroom window. I wolfed the mandatory breakfast, pulled on my corduroy pants, shirt and sneakers and galloped up the street.

Halfway to the lot I could hear the noise. They were playing ball. They were actually PLAYING BALL. It was unthinkable. I broke up the game.

"How come nobody yelled for me?" I shouted. "How come you guys started without me? Who's team am I on — what's the score? How come nobody came to GET ME?"

There were some giggles and a very smug look from Wilmer Davidson, Bubby's older brother. He was our best pitcher. "Because," he said very slowly, "YOU are a girl. And girls can't play ball."

I would like to say I punched him in the nose, then and there. I did not. I was stunned.

I knew I was a girl; they knew I was a girl; there had never been any question. It hadn't made any difference the day before, or the week or month or year before. It hadn't made any difference when I hit home runs or got somebody out, clean, at first base. It hadn't made any difference even when I did not get somebody out at first base. It made a difference that day, and would forever afterward. I knew it instantly.

The cat calls began. Girls swing like rusty gates. Go home and play with your dolls. I turned around and left the lot. I noticed that neither Shirley nor Beverly was around. I figured they had gotten the same treatment, and they had. There was no appeal.

I remember all of this now and can play it back in my mind as vividly as if it were some cinemascope, technicolor movie. I can taste the dust on my mouth and feel the sun on the back of my neck. I can feel the cheat in my belly. I was good, but I was a girl. No appeal.

It's the same cheat I felt in high school when the boys got the pool and the gym and the coaches who knew something. It's the cheat I felt seeing the boys in their letter sweaters, and the girls in their baggy, bloomer gym suits. Or, when I went to college and learned there was no such thing as a women's tennis team, although there was a men's team.

I did not and do not like the way that feels. I think we should all make sure it doesn't happen to our girl children.

Last week, when I discovered the University of Detroit is adding women's basketball and softball as varsity sports — complete with scholarships, tournaments and the whole bag — I stood up and cheered a little.

I did it in front of a fund-raising luncheon, and I'm doing it here now. I have no children in that school and no interest in Catholic education. But I have a burning, fighting-mad interest in giving girls, females, women every opportunity to be varsity athletes just like their brothers, fathers and husbands. Girls do not swing like rusty gates. And you can tell that to Wilmer Davidson the next time you see him.

— Nov. 13, 1977

I resent having an option too soon revoked

I wish Marvin Felheim didn't have to die right now. Sixty-three isn't old. He should live another 20 years in good health. A little arthritis or a slight hearing loss late in life would be OK. I could joke about that sort of thing.

Sometimes in his 80s or 90s is when Marvin Felheim should die. He should just pop off, unexpectedly, during an afternoon nap. It ought to happen on some cool, sunny day when the first of the roses begin to unfold in some garden near his house. A window ought to be open. He ought to be enjoying this sleepy hour, thinking about the next book he will write, or read.

His last conscious or semiconscious perceptions ought to be of the air, the faint scent of sun, earth and flowers, plus the softened sound of college kids laughing somewhere, heading down the street for the arboretum to drink beer and make love.

Just about then, some puffy, well-used artery in his head ought to blow — pooofff — and Marvin Felheim ought to sail out majestically, if confusedly, into whatever oblivion anti-world there may be.

That's how it ought to happen, but that is not how it is happening. Instead, this man I knew peripherally and briefly a couple of decades ago is dying right now, at age 63. He's been at it slowly and painfully for the past 10 years. He has bone cancer. By now the disease has pummeled him from his feet into a wheelchair and finally into his bed, where he survives on hardly more than chemicals and spirit. Perhaps spunk is a better word than spirit. It connotes some humor, some anger, some wisdom, mixed with stubbornness.

I hated reading about his hard times. A former classmate and sorority sister of mine from our University of Michigan days sent me a newspaper clipping detailing the agony and current thought of Marvin Felheim. It was a long, fine story which appeared in the Ann Arbor News, done with obvious respect for the man. I hated reading it anyway.

Marvin Felheim is a professor of English language and literature at U-M. He has been a teacher there for 31 years, ever since he earned a PhD from Harvard University and about two minutes later landed a job teaching English at the Harvard of the Midwest, which is what we like to call ourselves at U-M.

He arrived to teach shortly before I arrived to learn. We shared two or three classes. He was one of those rare teachers who made every classroom hour exciting, not merely tolerable. This made studying and the time spent preparing for the next hour a time of pleasant anticipation and willing effort. That's no easy trick for a teacher, and I can't really explain how he did it.

All we did in his class was what we did in other English classes. We read the assigned stuff. We talked in class about what we had read. Organization, structure, imagery, historical context and perspective, ideas, concepts. It was all a discovery process with this man, however. It was something like stalking saber-toothed tigers with him leading our expeditionary force. We were partners. He just carried the compass.

Often at the end of a class hour, the discussion would be so lively that we were obviously sorry time was up. Mr. Felheim, which is what he was called before he won his professor stripes, frequently said he'd be happy to hang around for another half hour if anybody wanted to continue. Sometimes he suggested we adjourn to a joint across the street for coffee, and more talk. Lots of us did this, lots of times. It was fun. Fun! Ridiculous.

It was never suggested that Marvin Felheim accumulated his academic groupies — which comprised both sexes, incidentally — because of his smashing good looks or his polished social manner.

He was tall, skinny, all elbows and knees, with a large nose and ears which protruded farther than handsome from the sides of his head. He wore heavy horn-rimmed glasses.

I watched him balancing a cup and saucer awkwardly on his knee at a sorority tea one Sunday afternoon. He looked out of plumb. In horror I saw the housemother moving his way. I knew he would attempt to stand, spewing tea and china all over both of them. Or, worse, he wouldn't stand. I was pleased to see a nearby sister smoothly remove the cup and saucer, saying she could tell he needed more, just in time for him to uncurl his ankles, unlock his knees, stand and shake hands with the dame fatale. He looked flustered, but grateful.

Marvin Felheim is all wound up in my growing up. He was learning to be a professor when I was learning to be a person. He was teaching me to love writing before I knew I wanted to write. He was kind and warmly accepting of almost everyone when I was cool and critical of almost everyone.

I have not seen this man or written him or had any communication with him for many, many years. I have always known I could, however. He was just 40 miles away. I resent having that option too soon revoked. Otherwise, I cannot explain the combination of sorrow and outrage I feel now.

His death won't change my life. His life changed mine, however, and maybe I rage against myself and the idea that I never drove over to Ann Arbor and told him how important he was to me, so that we could rejoice over it as if we had just discovered some hidden metaphor in a Yeats poem. There are times to acknowledge such things, and I missed it.

— May 18, 1979

Do the children remember how tired their mother was?

On Mother's Day, I think I'll ask the kids what they remember about me. It is not that I have vanished from their lives or they from mine. We're all still in the neighborhood. We see each other regularly and otherwise keep in touch by telephone. But, I'll ask anyway.

That's because the kids are pretty well grown up now. It's been a long time since I bought new chinos and tennies for them, in ever larger sizes. I lost the battle with Suzanne about piercing her ears so long ago I have forgotten now why I was so passionately opposed. Chuck no longer climbs trees just to pretend he is a bird. Jim no longer scrounges through neighbors' trash looking for discarded electric motors and other "good stuff" to tear down and rebuild.

The kids are pretty well grown up . . . and so am I.

I don't know when I grew up. I was still a child when my children were born. I didn't think so at the time. In retrospect, however, I know it is painfully true. In many ways, those early years now seem like a game in which I played Mommy and they played Babies, and while they came naturally to their parts I was frequently unsure of my lines and stage business.

What I remember about those years of intense "mothering" must be quite different from what they remember. Mostly I remember being so tired so much of the time.

There was this standard of wifely and maternal performance gleaned from the movies and the pages of House Beautiful magazine. It nagged at me and, being a child and inexperienced in such matters, I foolishly pursued the mirage:

Mommy was to be surrounded by flowers, beautiful furnishings and highly polished surfaces. There was never to be any clutter or mess. The children were to be beautifully dressed and always playing happily at quiet games. Mommy was to be relaxed and lovely. Still, she must always be ready to bake a cake, play a game, read a story, kiss a hurt, fix a broken toy and whip up Daddy's favorite dinner as effortlessly as she might whip up her own bubble bath — something she did regularly because there was always plenty of time and privacy for such modest personal indulgences.

What time? What privacy? What flowers and gleaming surfaces? None of it worked or happened. I remember being so tired so much of the time.

I wonder if I was too tired to have fun. I played the games and baked the cakes. Did I smile and laugh? Did I worry too much about laundry and about not making messes? I can't remember. Maybe the kids will.

I do remember sitting in the dark beside my daughter's bed and singing "Over the Rainbow" very softly to her almost every night. It was her lullaby. She loved it and asked for it, and I liked singing it, as much for myself as for her.

For Suzanne, the song belonged to Dorothy in "The Wizard of Oz," and it evoked all the images of that beloved story. It was about finding home-sweet-home. " . . . if happy little bluebirds fly beyond the rainbow, why, oh why can't I?" At the end, Suzanne always smiled and hugged and slept content that she was in her home-sweet-home.

For me, the mother-child enslaved by her own foolish fantasy of perfection, that song became one of bondage and longed-for release. Funny how it worked so well for both of us.

The boys wanted stories at bedtime but not the sort you read from books. They wanted them made up, and full of surprising twists and unexpected adventure. I did those too, stories about remarkable escapes from captivity and danger. I know we laughed together at those stories and sometimes changed the endings around two or three times until Chuck and Jim were satisfied they made sense. Sense? Fine nonsense, ending in yawns and sleepy hugs.

I will ask the kids what they remember of me when we were all children together. I hope they don't remember just and only that I was so tired so much of the time.

— May 10, 1981

I think everybody needs a kicking pan

I used to kick a pan around the basement. It was a small yellow, enameled roaster. By the time I tossed it in the trash, a couple of years after I took to kicking it, most of the enamel had chipped off, and what was left comprised a collection of metal bulges and dents.

I still remember the lovely crashing sound this pan made as it exploded against the concrete basement walls and clattered around on the tiled floor. I still remember how the lead weight in my belly and the invisible choke collar I wore at pan-kicking time lightened and loosened with every clatter and crash.

My children and I owe a lot to this battered chunk of metal, although it was part of their lives only a short period of time. Actually, it was hardly a part of their lives at all; just mine. Without the pan to abuse, I might have abused the kids. I felt it; I knew it, without thinking it through.

I'll not plumb all the problems. It is sufficient for this purpose that you know I was living in a small house with a corporate-ladder-climbing husband preoccupied with the ascent, plus three toddlers. These latter three were extremely inventive and energetic. In retrospect, there was too much work, too little rest, and I had fallen victim to the dreaded Doris Day syndrome.

This means that I believed there was such a thing as a perfect homemaker-wife-mother, and I could be IT. All I had to do was maintain a germ-free household suitable for display on the cover of House Beautiful magazine, cook like Duglass Duglass, be ever lovely as Loretta Young and manage the kids with the skill of a combination Hazel and Dr. Spock. If I could just do these simple things, at the same time eschewing all argument and being ever ready to subordinate my needs to those of others, I would achieve domestic bliss. This is the state of nirvana, for women.

I tried, and it made me miserable. I was constantly disappointed, frustrated and very lonely. The worse I felt, the more confused I became, because, damn it, I was trying, according to the book. Doris Day, however, never blows . . . except . . . except . . .

Fury demands ventilation. I was aware that something needed

smashing, and I was afraid too, because I knew that my own fury had nowhere to go, except toward the kids. They were handy, and little.

One more spilled glass of orange juice, one more rip in the new pair of jeans, one more blemish on the illusive castle in the air I was trying so hard to build, and somebody is going to get it!

I can't tell you why somebody didn't. I don't know what switch clicked inside my head. I do remember the day I grabbed the pan.

Suzanne, then age three, had just tossed some food which she found offensive — I think it was sliced beets — off her plate onto the kitchen floor. Splat! My urge was to toss her out a window. Instead, I grabbed the pan, headed for the basement and kicked it very hard against the wall. It was no thought-out act. It was instinctive and irrational. It felt good. I kicked it again. It felt wonderful. It made a terrible racket.

Pretty soon I came upstairs to face three wide-eyed babies standing in the kitchen. By now I felt a little silly, but much better, no more choke collar. I could even smile, though I figured from the way one toe on my right foot ached that I might have broken something.

I gathered the children around and told them that nothing seemed to be going right for me right now and that this made me very angry and that I didn't want to break anything important or hurt anyone, but I felt like breaking or hurting something. So I kicked this old pan around down there where it couldn't hurt anything, and now I feel better. Let's clean up the beets. Which we did.

That's how it went. My kicking pan became an "in" family joke. Sometimes when I got grouchy, one of the kids would fetch it for me. I used it from time to time during the next couple of years, after which I got courageous and smart enough to kick the Doris Day syndrome instead.

I think everybody needs a kicking pan sometimes. Maybe some people can exercise their need to pound on the golf course or tennis court. I read once that walloping a golf ball 350 yards or executing a perfect overhead smash is supposed to accomplish the same thing. I don't believe it. Someone who is as close to out-of-control as I was the day the pan rescued me is in no shape to play golf or tennis and abide by rules. What is needed is something to smash. Pounding a punching bag might work. A pillow is too soft and yielding; besides it doesn't make noise. Chopping wood might do it.

I don't know what shrinks call this business of dumping fury on something you can't hurt, instead of using it on something you can hurt. I know it's healthy, however. It is a whole lot more healthy than trying to "control yourself" when you have lost control.

I read recently of a man who shot a hardware-store owner and another man who happened to be in the store at the time, all because the hardware store owner didn't have a bicycle part the gunman wanted to buy. My managing editor tells a story of two neighbors in a Detroit suburb who couldn't agree on the kind of grass to plant in their adjoining yards. When one planted bent grass, and it began to spread into the Kentucky bluegrass planted by the other, the bluegrass neighbor shot and killed the bent-grass neighbor. At a newspaper, you hear lots of such stories. Kicking pans are useful, if not essential, to mental health. If you don't have one, you might want to figure one out for yourself. If you have never needed one, you're lucky.

— Sept. 22, 1978

A bittersweet time
for Jim and me

He was four years old and I was 32 when we met. His name was Tommy. I have mercifully forgotten his last name.

He was a small lump in a big bed with crib sides at St. Joseph Mercy Hospital in Pontiac. He was dying of leukemia. I knew him for four days.

Tommy was propped into a semi-sitting position with several pillows. Plastic tubes were dripping fluids into tiny arms and legs. He looked frail, very small for his age. His skin was a strange color, but he had large, wet eyes the color of milk chocolate. He didn't speak or move. Those enormous eyes tracked us into the room.

I had brought my own otherwise healthy son Jim, who was six then, to the hospital for hemstitching of a hernia acquired who knows how — climbing trees, falling off bicycles, wrestling with his brother. (My mother called the boys "active youngsters.")

Jim was apprehensive. I had assured him he would have another kid for a roommate, that his dad and I would visit lots, that I would bake brownies and bring them in and that after a bellyache for a few days he would feel fine. He was still apprehensive.

"Is that the kid?" Jim asked with that you've-put-one-over-on-me look. He's sick." It was obvious to Jim this would be no romp in the park.

"Yup. Well, let's say hello." It was obvious to me, too.

With some coaxing Tommy whispered his name. That was all.

During the next four days we got to know each other very well. I spent a lot of time in that small room talking to two boys, one healthy though hurting, one near death. I started out in a proper mother position, sitting in the visitor's chair near my son's bed. That quickly changed.

"Lady," Tommy whispered every day when I arrived. "Sit here." His eyes would move to the visitor's chair beside his bed. The eyes were all that Tommy moved. I never knew if he was in pain or if he simply had no energy to use his head or arms or body. It didn't matter.

Jim agreed it was OK for me to do what Tommy wanted because

Tommy was "really sick" and "a good kid." I assumed a position between them, but closer to Tommy's bed.

On Day Two Jim was groggy, but he began talking for Tommy. "Tommy wants a drink of water." I got the glass and straw. "Tommy wants you to see his new red car, at the foot of his bed." I pronounced it wonderful. "Tommy wants you to read us about the barberry bushes."

In Helen Beatrix Potter's original "Peter Rabbit" there is a line about how the coat buttons on Peter's jacket "inadvertently became entangled in the barberry bushes." It is delicious language. Neither boy had the sneakiest notion what the big words meant, but they liked the sounds. Jim always giggled. Tommy smiled — a rare occurrence.

That's how it went. Tommy took me over, with Jim's help.

"Lady, feed me." He could eat little, a bit of Jello, a spoonful of mashed potatoes. He was unable to feed himself. Whenever Tommy wanted to eat, he ate. There were no mealtimes for him and whenever I was there, it was mealtime.

Jim talked for Tommy and had one-way kid conversations with him about bikes and big sisters, kindergarten and first grade — neither of which Tommy would ever see. I followed whispered directions.

Jim told me that when the little furrows showed up on Tommy's forehead it meant he was uncomfortable and it was time for us, or a nurse, to gingerly change his body position. It was done. I don't know how Jim understood this. Tommy never whimpered.

One day, as I was reading about little Cindy Lou who was just barely two, Tommy whispered, "Lady, touch me." There should have been a harp arpeggio. Jim frowned. I was immobilized. We both knew that Tommy's skin was so sensitive that the slightest pressure, from a sheet or a pillow, was painful to him. He cringed during those body turnings. But he wanted that touch, and he was ready to feel the pain.

I rested my clumsy, grown-up fingertips as lightly as I could on one tiny hand, and I kept on reading. My voice was never so unsteady, and very soon I took my hand away because I knew it was hurting.

There were four days like this. Each was a bittersweet time for Jim and me. Then we went home. I think that was when I forgot Tommy's last name.

If I had remembered I would have followed his fading glory to its end. I would have taken on a larger measure of guilt (why do we do that?) and sorrow and sense of irretrievable loss than I could have absorbed. It would have made me sick. Sometimes our minds save us without rational help at all. I forgot Tommy's last name.

Jim was back climbing trees and falling off bicycles and wrestling with his brother in a few weeks. He told everybody at home and at school about his hospital stay and about his largely silent, immobile friend. With six-year-old directness he announced one day, "Tommy's probably dead now. He was great!"

A woman called a month ago to ask if I would donate something that might reflect my work or interests to a fund-raising garage sale planned by the Children's Leukemia Foundation of Michigan for the last week in April. For chrissake, I thought. I don't have anything like that.

"Yes, ma'am. I have a two-volume, biography of William Faulkner, whom I consider America's greatest writer (so far), written by a professor at the University of Michigan, which I consider America's greatest university (so far). It's yours, with my best wishes." I'd rather keep it. It's yours because of a love affair I had once a long time ago with a much younger man.

— April 22, 1977

No matter how you slice it, the cake goes on the floor

Infancy ends and childhood begins at about age five. In contemporary society, this important transition is frequently marked by a celebration known as the Terrible Birthday Party.

Mothers say to their friends, "I would love to go shopping on Wednesday, Shirley, but I've got this terrible birthday party planned for Bobby." Or it's, "We are not planning anything for Saturday night, Charlie. We're staying home and eating TV dinners. We're having that terrible birthday party on Saturday afternoon, you remember."

It is not that the fifth birthday party is planned to be terrible or even that it turns out to be a failure. That is not usually true. It is not usually a total disaster. It is not that parents resent organizing a party for their children either. It is just that the fifth birthday party strikes real terror into the heart of any thinking parent and especially mothers. They're the ones who do most of the planning, supervising and cleaning up.

Earlier birthday parties are easy. You invite the grandparents plus an uncle or an aunt or two. You fix sloppy joes and a salad, bake a cake, buy some film for the camera, and you're all set. For the first couple of years the honoree doesn't even know what a birthday is. He or she does not expect presents and is supremely uncritical of any which are offered. The little adorable toddles from hugger to hugger and generally falls asleep just before or soon after the singing of "Happy Birthday to You," with or without a brief spate of tears. When this happens, all the grown-ups continue to chatter and eat cake and have a fine time.

The Terrible Birthday Party is different. Other little kids are invited. Sometimes there are as many as a dozen. Most of them are total strangers to you; they are kids your own child has met in kindergarten. All the guests bring presents and the honoree expects every present will be wonderful. (A 50 percent disappointment rate is guaranteed.) The revelers all expect funny hats to wear, wonderful things to eat and drink, exciting games to play, and terrific prizes to win and take home with them. (A 50 percent disappointment rate is guaranteed.)

The mother of the honoree expects all the wee ones to arrive and depart according to the hours noted on the invitation, be orderly, polite, pleasant-tempered and extremely neat. (A 100 percent disappointment rate is guaranteed.)

The father of the honoree expects to play golf all afternoon. He usually does. (That's a 100 percent satisfaction rate.) He typically arrives home 10 minutes after the last house ape has been collected by his or her parent, one full hour after everyone else has left. Father wants to know what happened to the reading lamp in the family room which was fine this morning but is now broken, and when to expect dinner.

After dinner or the next day, the grandmothers call. They ask, "How was the birthday party?" Mother says, "Terrible!" She details the running around, the arguing, the falling down, the throwing up, the hysterical laughter, the grinding of cake with butter cream icing into the new carpet in the family room and how the lamp got smashed when Bobby and his best friend got into a tug-of-war with the sash from Mary Ellen Baldwin's dress . . . which ripped . . . which made Mary Ellen cry . . . which started a shoving match between Bobby and Mary Ellen after Bobby called her a cry baby.

Grandmothers then ask to talk to the birthday kid. They ask, "How was the party?" The birthday child says, "It was OK." Grandmothers usually wonder if it was "fun" or "exciting." It is sometimes pronounced "sort of fun," but mostly the five-year-old critic says it was simply "OK," which is usually a very generous review, all things considered.

There are certain cardinal rules to remember if you are planning a Terrible Birthday Party. They are:

• Color match all liquid refreshments with the family room rug. Cola goes well only with dark brown shag. Seven-Up is a good, all-area choice. Red pop, red punch and any concoction cleverly gussied up with food coloring are to be avoided no matter what. That which spills on the carpet stays on the carpet, is the rule. Everything will spill.

• Attempt to color-match the cake and frosting to the carpet as well. This is sometimes difficult. A slate gray cake with gray icing is hard to special order. Come as close as you can. Make sure this cake is covered with frosting rosebuds. Every child at the party will want several rosebuds on his or her cake slice. The birthday child will want more than anybody else. Nobody will eat any of them.

• Never serve any carbonated beverage in the bottle. Shake 'em, squirt 'em battles inevitably follow.

• Do not give bubble-blowing equipment as prizes. The little jars of bubble stuff will also be spilled. Finger paints are ditto, and worse. Do not give horns or whistles either, unless all adults have been issued ear plugs.

• If paper hats or crowns are to be worn by party guests, be sure to buy some large stick-on decorations for the headgear of the birthday child. Day-glo red, orange, blue, gold and silver stars are recommended, in any combination. Big ones. The honoree will want no confusion about who is Big Magilla.

• If possible, designate separate boys' and girls' lavatories. This will cut down significantly on squeals, screams and door slammings, although they cannot be eliminated totally.

• Send all dogs, cats and other common pets for which you care to the kennel for the day. If there is a pet snake in the house, a gerbil family, any lizards, salamanders, frogs or toads, any rabbits, ducklings or guinea pigs and especially if there is a spider collection, lock it or them all together in a room before any guests arrive. Hide the key. Refuse all whining pleas to tell where it is. Pray.

— *March 31, 1980*

An imaginary family
can be mourned, too

The dollhouse was beloved. It stood on the floor, under a low, sunny window in Suzanne's bedroom. When she was four and five and six years old, the tiny doll family which lived in the house was frantically busy.

Mother did a lot of cooking, as I recall, and was otherwise preoccupied tending a tiny baby, bundled in a patch of flannel and tucked into a cradle. Father sat in the living room reading, and he frequently came and went from and to "work," which was a mysterious place across the room on Sue's bed. The brother and sister dolls, trailed by a puppy, were forever running upstairs and downstairs, climbing onto the roof, getting lost, being found, getting sick, getting well, having vicious physical battles and making up with tender hugs and kisses. Suzanne manipulated this tiny family and gave it vibrant life, drawn from her own.

The doll family, strangely I thought at the time, had no name. It was not some obscure family of Joneses or exotic collection of Gumbogglewigs. Sue told me quite forcefully, in response to my question one day, that the dolls were definitely not McWhirters. "They're people," she said — and that was that.

The dolls were universals. This explained perfectly their absence of sur- or given names, labels which would have set them apart from the rest of humankind. The dolls were simply Father, Mother, Brother, Sister, Baby and Puppy, archetypical and eternal. But I knew they were also McWhirters, because my child had little experience with universals during her first handful of years. Listening in on dollhouse conversation, I learned a great deal about the world as it seemed to be, and perhaps was, for a small child.

Whenever Mother was particularly carping and repressive, I knew it was time for me to take a look at my own behavior and make appropriate revisions. Whenever Father disappeared from the scenario for a day or two, I knew it was time for Ed to think about a Lego building project or reading the bedtime stories again. If Brother and Sister were constantly bickering and shoving each other down the stairs, I figured the balance of power and affection between

Sue and her brothers might be wavering and I should probably think about a possible remedy.

Mostly, however, Suzanne's universal family romped happily and predictably through its make-believe world and this was a pleasant, if blatantly male chauvinist, place.

Mother and Father discussed things but Father made all the important decisions. There were few family arguments. Mother tended to household chores and clucked a lot. She was trusting and gullible. He was strong and protective. Both parents scolded, but rarely punished harshly.

Baby and Puppy got into dangerous situations and had to be rescued. Brother and Sister were the hero and heroine, snatching Puppy and Baby from the jaws of death, or worse. Worse was being lost.

This happened frequently to Puppy and required spooky searches by Brother and Sister through dark woods (a philodendron plant) or strange neighborhoods (under the bed). Another frequent calamity involved family members falling down the stairs or off the roof. Terrible injuries resulted from these spills, but universal family members always recovered fully, after brief bed rest.

The dollhouse world was simple and loving and exciting. I had forgotten all about it, until last week.

I decided to clean the basement. This is sometimes a dangerous enterprise, as I discovered. In a dusty corner, under a sheet long ago relegated to rag status, I rediscovered the dollhouse. It took me by surprise and for a minute I could only stare at it, as if it were some ghost and ominous presence from another planet.

Everything was there — Mother, Father, Sister, Brother, Puppy and Baby, plus all the furniture, the tiny dishes, the faded snips and pieces of fabric which served as blankets and table linens. Over it all was a fine sifting of dust and grime. The furniture was scattered and overturned. Family members lay in awkward poses, separate, disengaged and lifeless. They were dead, dead as oak leaves rattling in a winter wind. I wept, and most ungracefully, too.

How can one mourn the death of an imaginary family? How can one feel outrage and fury and guilt and sorrow all at once over something so insignificant as an abandoned outgrown dollhouse and its universal family? That's how I felt.

Then I knew it was because this family was not universal at all. It was an extension of my own family and the fanciful creation of my own child. The dollhouse and its family were and are us, in some mystic way. To let it disintegrate would be . . . outrageous? Of course. Unthinkable!

So I will clean and polish the dollhouse, redecorate it, sponge off Mother, Father, Sister, Brother, Baby and Puppy, repair their clothes and set things right in that tiny household. Then I'll cover it all up again, more carefully this time, and wait. I expect that Suzanne will reclaim it one day for some child of her own to enliven. If not, I will give it to an appropriate small person, kin or no kin. This, too, is immortality.

— May 10, 1978

Nothing embarrasses more than a parent who dances

Enid Nemy of the New York Times wrote recently and humorously of the gross embarrassment parents cause their kids. If your mother made you wear leggings to school for example, when everyone else got to shiver at the bus stop in nothing more than bare legs and bobby socks, didn't you just die! Nemy cataloged some of the horrors of childhood mortification as remembered by various persons she knows. Some things change but these never do.

There is having to play the piano, dance or recite for strange adults; having to introduce your friends to a relative who speaks no English; having to listen as your father or your mother tells some store clerk every single, agonizing detail of why you need a new suit or dress. It's stuff like that.

My father used to embarrass me by burying his nose in a book or magazine the minute any of my friends, and especially a boyfriend, arrived at our house. My father was not a particularly quiet man within the bosom of his family. He always had plenty to say about everything. In the presence of strangers under the age of 25, however, he was suddenly struck dumb and seized by some compulsion to devour the New Yorker, cover to cover, topped off by six chapters of War and Peace.

I hated that. I thought everybody I knew would think my father was weird. If he had blathered like a carnival pitch man I would have been equally embarrassed, however. I know that because I was also embarrassed by my mother, a friendly and congenial person, who I thought talked entirely too much. There is no pleasing kids.

When my daughter Suzanne was about 13 and a junior high school student, her father and I received a telephone call from someone at the school asking if we would chaperone a school dance. It was to be the premiere social event of the junior high season. That meant the dance would be in the evening, rather than the afternoon, and there would be a live band. Of course, we accepted.

"Oh, noooooo!" moaned our daughter. "I'll be soooooo embarrassed."

"What's wrong with us?" said her father, naively. "We clean up pretty well. We don't spit on the floor. We even know how to dance."

"Don't dance!" Sue ordered. "If you are going to chaperone my dance, I get to set the rules. OK?"

OK. She did.

Not only were we forbidden to dance together, we were forbidden to dance at all. "Even if the principal invites you to dance, Mom, promise me you won't." I promised. I said I would make up a story about having a sprained knee and seven broken toes. She said that would be fine.

Sue reserved the right to choose the clothing Ed and I would wear to this gala, " . . . so you won't look too gross." She also wanted the right of first refusal on her mother's hair style and choice of jewelry, if any.

She told Ed and me we were not to approach her or speak to her directly at anytime during the course of the evening. We might smile at her. Once. We were similarly warned not to converse with any of her friends or any other kids, whether we knew them or not.

She would be transported to and from the party by the father of a girlfriend, as previously planned. It did not matter that the family car containing her adoring parents would be making the same trips. She would rather die than arrive at or leave the dance in the same car with her parents.

I can't remember the exact circumstances but I know I never got to that dance. I may have contracted bubonic plague. Maybe I had to work. At any rate, I missed it. Ed fulfilled our chaperone duty. He bent or broke most of the rules.

He danced, not only with a teacher or two but with one or two of the girls, many of whom we had known since their diaper days. He actually spoke to several kids. He said he had a pretty good time, altogether, deducting points for the electric guitars and the fact that the punch definitely suffered for lack of vodka.

Sue was iffy on his performance. "He wasn't too terrible," she admitted. One of her girlfriends had even told her, "Your dad's kind of nice." That's the only thing that saved him.

It is impossible to be an admirable parent during the decade between your child's 10th and 20th birthdays. The best you can hope for is not being too terrible.

You are always too skinny or too fat, too short or too tall, too gabby or not nearly gabby enough. Your clothes are never right. You dance funny. The things you like to do are never any fun. The topics you choose to talk about are invariably "dumb."

Miraculously, most parental shortcomings seem to disappear or improve dramatically as the child grows older. Sometimes parents are even forgiven and recognized as the decent human beings most of them are.

I don't know how long it takes. Maybe as long as it takes for the child to grow up, have a baby or two of his or her own and begin to hear that, "Oh, noooooo! I'm so embarrassed," from the next generation. I can hardly wait.

— *Feb. 24, 1980*

Bless the salamanders, too — God understands

In an earlier life, when the McWhirter children were still children and our house was full of three generations of blood kin for all holiday feasts, I didn't always devote sufficient time to careful planning.

That was how it happened that one Thanksgiving Day long past, Ed McWhirter turned to our son, Charlie (Frick of Frick & Frack fame) and asked if he would like to offer thanks.

"Huh?" said Charlie dully, eyes fixed on the turkey awaiting the knife.

"Offer the prayer," Ed coached.

"Oh," said his eminence. "Bow your heads and close your eyes . . ." Fourteen people complied.

" . . . Thank you for the turkey. Amen," Charlie said.

There were giggles all around. It might have been best to leave it there, but Ed decided the occasion demanded more pomp and piety.

"You can do better," he told Charlie. "We have more to be thankful for than turkey."

"I'll do it" said Jim. He's Frack, Charlie's twin brother, ever eager to demonstrate that anything Frick can do, Frack can do better. "Bow your heads and close your eyes . . . "

We did, again.

The King James version.

"Dear God," began King James. "Thank you for the turkey, and the mashed potatoes, and the salad . . .

"Save us" I whispered to Ed. "He's going to mention everything on the table."

"mmmmm," Ed mmmmed.

" . . . and the celery, and the rolls, and the silverware, and the dishes, and the tablecloth . . . "

Grandmothers began to fidget. Cousins giggled. Suzanne, sister of Frick & Frack, laughed out loud when King James got to " . . . and our dog Muffin, and the apple tree in the backyard, and my bicycle and . . . "

"The gravy's getting cold," I hissed to Ed.

" . . . and the frog I caught in the creek," intoned King James, "and the salamanders, and the empty lot where we play baseball, and my baseball cards and . . . "

And there's more.

The Thanksgiving blessing had by now consumed perhaps five minutes and King James showed no sign of exhausting that for which he could give thanks. No heads were bowed any longer. Everyone was staring at our religious leader and the children were convulsed in laughter.

"Oh, no" shrieked Charlie at each new category of persons, places or things for which his brother was offering up his most pious gratitude. King James had a grin on his face which threatened to erupt into a belly laugh from time to time, but he somehow managed to control it as he kept his hands prayerfully together and continued his fervent paean of praise.

"OK, everybody," Ed said finally, "Amen."

"Amen," we chorused.

"Well, amen," sighed King James, "but I had lots more to go."

After that, I made sure to assign table prayer duty to someone a few days ahead of time. It was always one of the children. He or she was told to keep it brief, and applicable to all. We had no further surprising religious experiences.

It's odd, though. The only prayer I remember out of dozens offered over many years is that spontaneous one of Jim's in which he thanked God for salamanders and baseball cards — and had lots more to go when we turned him off. When I count my blessings, I include that day. I marvel at the understanding of a child who knew what blessings are all about, and who had collected so many after a mere seven or eight years on earth.

— Nov. 11, 1983

Life is full of surprises, but few come gift-wrapped

The woman was married for 20 years. Every summer when her birthday loomed on the June horizon, her family planned a celebration. It never changed.

The immediate family gathered, always at this woman's own home. Her husband stoked the outdoor grill with charcoal and fretted over steaks or hamburgers, depending on the state of the family budget. There were the predictable and simple accompaniments — sliced tomatoes, potato salad, fruits — usually bought at a delicatessen and heaped into bowls by the children.

In the early years, there was likely to be a home-baked cake, supplied by a grandmother. As time passed, however, it seemed easier to buy a cake at the local supermarket or bakery. The cake was suitable for any person of any age. It always said, "Happy Birthday" in green or yellow icing, with rosebuds and leaf swirls.

"Happy Birthday to yooouu . . . Happy Birthday to yooouu . . ." the ritual choruses were sung. Candles, never presenting her true age because the cake top couldn't accommodate the growing number, were huffed out. The woman made a wish first. It was always the same: "Please, let me find contentment in my life this year." She never told what she wished. It ruined the magic to tell, she said, and everyone laughed and agreed that was so.

After the wish and the candles, there were presents. Blouses and summer skirts or shorts of some kind were popular choices of the gift givers. The husband sometimes offered utilitarian items. There was a new corn popper one year and a coffee maker another time. The woman had said she needed these things for the kitchen.

The gifts were always useful and attractive and never extravagant or frivolous. The children were pleased if she was pleased. The husband was pleased if she was pleased. She was always very pleased.

Every year after the gift opening, the woman took a secret moment to look around at this gathering of her blood and note how much she loved each one, personally, individually, for all kinds of reasons and for no reasons whatsoever. Sometimes she had tears in her eyes and explained them away by laughing and saying it was just that she was a marshmallow, a sentimental softie. Sometimes she excused herself and went into a bathroom and sobbed quietly for a few minutes, after which she put drops in her reddened eyes, wiped away the streaks on her cheeks and rejoined her family, always smiling. She never told anyone about the crying.

The tears were for love, but not purely so. Those tears mingled with tears of disappointment, confusion, sorrow and depression. "I do not understand, Lord," she prayed once, "why these people I serve and love so very much never, never celebrate me. This birthday is my one day a year. That's what birthdays are about. Why is my being on this earth cause for such joyless observance? It is always duty, and routine. Am I never to have a joyful surprise, lovingly planned and kept?"

Then she felt guilty and selfish. Later and often she prayed, "Lord, help me to be more worthy of their love and yours, help me to be less selfish and to do your work and be content with that." This was what she had been taught to pray.

The contentment never came.

Reinforced by birthday after birthday filled with store-bought cake and predictable ritual, she grew to hate the annual observance of herself. It reminded her over and over again, lest she get uppity and forget, that persons who knew and loved her best had long ago decided that coffee pots and hamburger were suitable recognition of her worth.

Gala parties, extravagant or imaginative presents, tender testimonials of love and all other happy surprises came to other, more deserving people on their special days. She rejoiced over many years for assorted friends and neighbors whenever one of them, man or woman, was so honored. And, she grieved secretly and guiltily for herself. "Selfish! Selfish!" she told herself, but the self-criticism didn't make her content.

If this were a made-up story, I would end it with some miraculous enlightenment visiting itself on the heart and mind of the husband. I would say his inspiration radiated to other family members and resulted in a spectacular surprise celebration of some sort which restored this woman's self-esteem and washed away the decades of self-pity, depression and hopeless yearning. It would be fantasy. Life is not so romantic or forgiving.

Nothing at all happened to these people until the woman learned a lesson no one had suggested to her. You get what you ask for. If you ask to be a doormat, you are so treated. If you ask to be celebrated, you get a celebration.

If you would be content, you must devise your own contentment, and if you would be happy, you must create your own happiness. No person is responsible for these things except you. No action or inaction of another person or persons can give joy or pain unless you invite it and encourage it.

Once the woman discovered these things, she realized the cookouts would have served as well as the gala parties, if she had let them, and that if she had wanted a spree, she could have planned it herself, to everyone's pleasure. She felt dumb, but relieved, and strangely, mysteriously, content.

— June 25, 1979

The wedding date's set;
now the divorce is final

There is a wedding being planned for mid-December, to which I will not be invited. Nor should I be. The occasion will not go unmarked on my personal calendar, however.

Ed McWhirter, former husband of mine and forever father of three children who comprise equal parts him and me, is marrying again. Dingdong, the bells are going to chime.

The impending nuptials have been much on my mind, for many reasons. First, everyone from the kids to my friends who have never laid eyes on Ed has pressed me with the same question: "How do you feel about that?" It seems important for them to know. Second, even if no one else knew that this man were about to take a second wife, I would be forced to press the question on myself: "How do you feel about that?"

In California, I read, 80 percent of first marriages end in divorce. Nationally, it's one divorce for every two marriages in recent years. Most of the men, if not the women, remarry.

What I feel, then, can't be much different from emotions shared by many other people, of both sexes. I'd like to believe myself supremely unique, but I know I am similar to others. Maybe if I sort out some of these emotions, the exercise may be informative, or useful, considering we never know who's going to wander into this unfamiliar neighborhood on any given day.

There is a release from guilt. Isn't that odd? I never consciously felt guilty. Now I feel the relief so I know I must have felt guilty.

That's probably because the divorce was my idea. I guess over the past several years I have felt vaguely responsible for Ed's loneliness, when I was aware of it, and for his awkwardness and sometime sadness, living as an unmarried person. He was never much of a cook and he always hated coming home to an empty house. Lords knows he had plenty of pleasant female companionships, but there were fallow times too. And some of the presumably warm relationships were much more convenience than romance, or so he frequently confided. We kept in touch.

Now there is this woman he plans to marry and who, one

presumes, is delighted to marry him. I can drop my guilt baggage. It is a relief, and I am genuinely happy for him, her and even me. But not totally.

What else do I feel? A little angry, a little jealous; considerably unsettled.

Emotions are never reasonable. We can't bid them come or go. They're mysterious forces which defy full explanations, Freud be hanged. We can only find clues.

Anger. Let's see: I did not then and do not now want to be married to this man, as I remember him in the not-so-good-old-days of our neurotic marriage. We are both different now, however. The divorce and the independence it thrust on each of us has been a crucible. We are both much more able to ask, give and share.

Maybe I'm angry because some other woman will reap the benefits of this painful maturation and learning process which I forced and which he and I both endured to our mutual benefit as human beings.

Maybe I am a real witch. Maybe I actually want him to remain unmarried as some sort of cruel punishment for real or imagined past affronts. Maybe I am willing to bear guilt in order to enjoy his misery. See, you terrible man, I don't want you and nobody else does either.

No, that's not it. I have never felt that Ed is rotten or terrible, nor have I enjoyed others' misery. I suspect the former explanation is closer to the root of this anger weed than the latter.

It probably accounts for the jealousy, too. The crucible of divorce, which we shared, and its effects on us, which we shared in many quiet conversations, seemed part of the whole process of marriage. It was not. It was a different process. We should have cut all of our ties long ago, but we didn't. We tried to keep what was good and throw away only the bad parts. Perhaps this is impossible.

This woman, whom I now emotionally perceive as an intruder on a very personal and private relationship, is not that at all. But I still wish she would go away. I am jealous. She is claiming as her own that small part of Ed which he still wanted to give and which I still wanted to receive.

"A divorce is never final until one party or the other remarries," she said. She is a divorced friend and associate. It doesn't matter who walks out or for what reason. It doesn't matter if you think he's an SOB and he can't stand the sight of you. Maybe one person lives in New York and one in China. Until one or the other gets married again, in your head it's always just a separation. The court papers don't mean a thing.

I remembered a woman who is now well past the age to collect Social Security. She had been divorced more than 20 years before the time of an incident she told me about. She was in a different city and sought out the street where her former husband lived. She saw him raking leaves in the yard. She said her heart started pounding and she was afraid she would have an attack of the vapors or something. "If he or I ever married again, I would never have looked for him or had any interest at all," she told me. "Isn't it funny? I don't know why I did it. I just wanted to see how he looked, I guess." I guess. Separation.

Well, the McWhirter separation is soon to be over and the divorce final. The confusion is in this melange of emotion and in the sure knowledge that all of our lives — Ed's and mine plus those of Sue, Chuck, Jim, the grandmothers and everyone who touched any of us — will change again. One more time.

Change can be joyful and good. The birth of a child bodes well. So should a marriage. It would be false to say I am untouched and unmoved by the news of his wedding to be, but I am working it out. I wish all of us peace, warmth, love and happy days. I also hope someone gets him to the church on time. He is notoriously late for everything.

— Nov. 19, 1978

My Christmas tree's loaded with significance

I spiffed up the house the other day and put up a Christmas tree. That's hardly worth mentioning, since a zillion people do the same thing every year about this time. This was a first for me, however, and it taught me things about myself — some good, some not so.

First, the not so: Dependency is subtle. I do not consider myself a dependent person. Yet, for more than five years — ever since the Mcwhirter marriage flamed out over Birmingham — I have ducked the Christmas tree issue.

I have decked my various halls with wreaths, garlands, baubles and bangles. Never a tree. Who needs it? I couldn't abide a plastic tree. The real thing is messy and heavy. How would I stand it up? What would I hang on its branches? Too much trouble. Pass the poinsettias, please.

Actually, lurking somewhere in my head was the real reason: terror. I was an innocent in the matter of Christmas tree engineering.

Back in the Second Ice Age when I was three feet tall and wore galoshes over my Mary Janes, I trotted along with Dear Old Dad to tree lots. He was the expert who knew how tall or fat our tree should be. He knew about the needles. Most important, he knew how to assess a tree trunk. Was it straight, gnarled or spindly? Would it fit our tree stand? I went along to pass aesthetic judgment and decide if the personality of the tree fit mine. (It always did.)

By the time I had kicked galoshes in favor of leather boots with stacked heels, there was Ed McWhirter to do all these things. Then, there were our kids to go along with their Dad to the lots, and I could stay at home. I usually did.

The men in the family dragged in the tree and performed whatever surgery was necessary to attach it to the tree stand. They stood the conifer in its corner, attached the lights and put the angel on her top perch. Sue and I hung baubles, made our aesthetic judgments and decided if the personality of the tree fit our family. (It always did.)

In retrospect, I knew nothing about choosing or erecting a Christmas tree, until last week. Dependency.

When I finally decided I could not enjoy another Christmas deprived of a tree, I considered alternatives. I could lean on my sons for their muscle. Other mothers do that. I could invite some male friend in to help. I could invite a half-dozen people and cook spaghetti and uncork a bottle of wine and call it a party. Anyway, I could round up some Daddy-Husband-Big Brother surrogates and let them solve the selection and engineering problems.

"Otherwise," thought I, "you will just have to go without, or do it yourself, you pansy."

I didn't like thinking of myself as a pansy. I did it myself. I did it for the adventure and the testing. It was very easy.

Now, why do you suppose it took me five years to screw up enough courage to try to put up a Christmas tree? Big deal, independent, bright, able-bodied female idiot, that's me. I was scared by a routine job I had seen done dozens of times by many persons of different ages, none of whom has any more sense or skill than I have. I was scared because I could always depend on somebody else for this job; I never had to try.

The good thing I learned is not to be afraid or dependent in this way again. I thought I already knew that, after racing cars and shooting river rapids in a raft. Then there were the times when my kids got me onto ski hills designed to maim, but I somehow cheated the hills. All of that is a different kind of testing, however.

The real test of self-esteem and independence comes in living a routine life courageously and zestfully. It is the person who has never picked up a paint brush deciding to paint the garage and do it properly, because if somebody else can do it, then she can. It is the person who has never boiled water deciding to whip up a chocolate souffle, and a beauty at that, because if somebody else can do it, then he can. It was me, putting up a Christmas tree. No big deal.

I suspect there are a dozen small, routine somethings in every life which every person would like to see done. It's always someone else's responsibility; it's someone else's skill which is needed. Piffle.

We underrate our abilities and overrate our inadequacies. Anything you can do, I can do — well, maybe not better or even as well. But I can do it! That Christmas tree has layers and layers of significance this year. Jingle Bells!

— Dec. 15, 1978

No 'bah, humbug' for me— I'm baking cookies this year

Something is definitely wrong. I keep staring out the window wishing I were at home, baking Christmas cookies. I don't usually bake Christmas cookies. I buy them. This is how I know something is wrong.

Where are my pre-Christmas blues? They always strike about this time. There is vague melancholia, accompanied by a backache from lugging packages through shopping centers. By now I have usually lost all my lists and energy, overdrawn my checking account, burst my budget and just realized that the Christmas cards I addressed last week are still sitting in a box in the guest room waiting for the stamps I forgot to buy. This tends to bring me down.

Most of the above has happened again this year, but the blues have not struck. I have not been tempted to say, "Bah, humbug!" even once, and I plan to bake the cookies. I think the difference has something to do with some very nice things which have happened quite unexpectedly this year.

First, there are filing-cabinet tops covered with cards sent by people who read my work. The cards have little notes penned inside, mostly telling me the card senders appreciate what I have tried to share with them. The idea that my name is on Christmas card lists of persons and families I have never met, and that some harried man or woman actually took time from the holiday scurry to send me a note is a very pleasant surprise. It's also humbling, and that suits the season.

Second, some kids rang my doorbell the other night and sang Christmas carols. They were a ragtag group, including some of the neighborhood pests, but they were all smiles and music. They looked beautiful and sounded angelic, if slightly off key. I gave them candy canes. That was when I decided I wanted to bake cookies.

I would hate to see carol-singing become the December equivalent of Halloween trick-or-treat, but it seemed that I should offer the carolers something to say "thank you" for the serenade.

It occurred to me that almost all of the music we consume along with our Christmas cheer comes from radios and record players.

Real, live human voices — even slightly off key — are much more beautiful than these recorded sounds. The carolers reminded me of that.

Finally, I got a phone call from my mother the other day. She was chipper and excited. "I have the most beautiful Christmas tree," she said. "It is the prettiest thing I have ever seen!" She said Bill Sanford had decorated it for her.

Bill Sanford does floral arrangements for some tres chic florist in the Renaissance Center. Mom has known him since he was Billy and about four feet tall. On a day off, Bill arrived at Mom's place and told her he was prepared to make a thing of beauty out of her tree, utilizing materials at hand plus his considerable skill at this sort of thing. He did, and stayed on for supper.

You should understand that Mom has arthritis and a very iffy heart. She has had cataract surgery and is still struggling to regain some of her vision. She has the spirit of a Caesar, but her warrior's body has been considerably weakened in battle. Trimming a tree loomed as the Alps.

Bill's gift of himself, his time and his talent was generous and loving. It was the perfect gift for him to give to this particular woman, and he understood that. So did she.

I thought about presents and how they can be something you buy in a store. When they are that alone, however, they aren't nearly as fine as something which carries a little bit of you along with it.

I remember laughing at my great aunts and uncles exchanging put-ups with friends and neighbors at Christmastime. Put-ups were things the aunts and uncles had put up themselves — jellies and jams, conserves, candied fruits. One of the uncles even made dandelion wine. I thought all this stuff was probably pretty good, but not much of a present compared with the jars and bottles in fancy boxes in the stores. I thought the old folks oohed and aahed too much over this homemade stuff.

Then one year my daughter, who is a much better seamstress than I, made a blue velvet vest and gave it to me for Christmas. It was very well made, and it fit! — miracle of all. I suppose she could have bought me a vest, and I suppose I would have been well pleased. Probably, by now, I would have worn it enough to relegate it to the giveaway box, and it would be forgotten.

Not the blue one. It is still in my closet and gets an occasional wearing. That's because every time I see it, this vision of Suzanne, the child seamstress, laboring at our cantankerous old sewing machine to make a present just for me pops into my head. I would be a fool to throw that vision away.

Thinking about these things has prevented the pre-Christmas blues and driven me, happily, to baking cookies. It's either that or write poems for everybody. They would probably be even more sugary. Cookies will do.

— Dec. 20, 1978

Time turns the ordinary into fascinating chronicles

Lorene is my mother; Suzanne is my daughter. It was Lorene's birthday last week, so Suzanne and I gathered her up and took her out for a cozy dinner celebration.

The table conversation turned to family, not those persons present or living, but those long dead, reaching back through many generations in all directions. Suzanne was insatiably curious.

"Tell me about her!" she said whenever a new name was mentioned. "Tell me about him!" Who were these great-grandparents and multiple great-grandparents? Where did they live? How did they live? What did they look like? What did their houses look like? What did these people do for fun? What were their good times and hard times?

Mom and I could tell Sue some things about her great-greats on our side of the genealogical chart. I knew them as old folks and as a child knows elderly relatives. My mother knew them old and younger, too, and from a more grown-up perspective.

Neither of us, however, could give this youngest female in our line much information at all about her progenitors three, four or five generations back, and we were woefully ignorant of her father's family history.

It was frustrating for all of us.

"Why didn't somebody write it all down?" wailed Suzanne. Nobody ever thought about it, I guess. Family history is mostly oral history and sketchy.

I remember Aunt Besse, a great-aunt of Ed McWhirter, my husband in a previous life and the father of curious Suzanne and her two brothers. When Aunt Besse was in her 80s, and the children were wiggly house apes, they used to squirm around on Bessie's couch after church on Sundays and pretend to listen as she told them about "the olden days."

Besse said she could dimly remember being a very young child and being driven in a buggy to the railroad station in the Ohio town where she lived. It was raining, and her mother wrapped Besse up in a heavy cape and put her under the fringed top of the buggy.

Most of the townspeople were there, watching the tracks in the rain, waiting for a train that finally appeared.

The men took their hats off in the rain, Besse said, and her father held her up and told her to look at the train and remember it. The train went by slowly and didn't stop, and then everyone went home.

Even though Besse was very young, she thought all of this rather odd, and later her mother explained the train had been President Lincoln's funeral train, taking his body home to Illinois for burial.

Aunt Besse talked often about a hat shop she owned in Ohio when she was a young woman. In the 1880s she designed and made great and glorious chapeau out of satins and velvets to match the gowns of semi-elegant Midwestern matrons.

She told about two- and three-day train trips to New York City to buy egret feathers and yards of imported fabrics, of packing food in a wicker basket to eat on her journey, of private compartments on the train and of the scandal it was for a young woman to travel alone.

She talked of great adventures she had in New York City, riding in carriages and going to elegant dancing parties she sometimes did not discuss back home in Ohio, where many people considered dancing just as sinful as traveling alone.

Aunt Besse talked about all these things while the kids wiggled and paid hardly any attention. Even Ed and I paid only polite attention. Then Besse died, and now Suzanne wants to know all about this stuff, and there is no one to ask except me, her father and the grandmothers, and all of us have only secondhand information in tiny fragments.

What a waste.

I envy people who have diaries and journals written by relatives many generations ago. Each life is history and adventure that will or would be fascinating to the generations to come. The trouble is that living seems so ordinary and uninteresting on any given Tuesday. Few of us bother to record anything about it for our kids' kids' kids. We should.

I could explain my IBM Selectric typewriter and this blinking Atex video display terminal I use for stringing together words. A couple of generations from now these electronic tools will seem as quaint and crude as quill pens. Maybe.

We could write letters to our kids' kids' kids describing our vacations and our home improvement projects. We could tell them about shopping centers and supermarkets and the frustrations of

Christmas shopping and roasting turkeys.

We might describe favorite movies, plays, TV shows and rock concerts. Anything and everything would be welcome three generations along the time warp. Whatever we record for our kids' kids' kids to read could be more fascinating for them than "War and Peace," more intimate than "Lady Chatterley's Lover."

I don't suppose we'll all take to writing journals and saving them and passing them along, but we should. Daily living seems so ordinary, as previously noted.

I presume that's what Cleopatra's handmaidens thought.

— Nov. 28, 1980

Charlie's commencement was a day of remembrance

Charlie told me it would take about three hours to drive approximately 165 miles between home and the Civic Auditorium where his college commencement ceremonies would take place. He said I should allow extra time because parking would be a problem. "And there aren't any reserved seats either," he said. "You don't want to have to stand."

He got that I-know-what-you're-thinking look on his face. "Mom," he said. "You don't really have to come to the commencement. I won't be mad or disappointed or anything. Really." He knew what I was thinking because my son knows me as well as anybody. He knows that sleeping until I wake up is my favorite way to spend any morning, especially Saturday. To get to this commencement ceremony, I would have to be dressed, and on the road by about 7 a.m.

"I want to be there," I said. He smiled. "It has taken five years and a million dollars to get you through college, and that doesn't count the wear and tear on my maternal worry system," I noted. "I'll be there." He smiled again.

That's why last Saturday I dragged myself out of bed and into the shower at 6 a.m. A heavy gray fog was rolling off Lake St. Clair. It was already oppressively hot and promising to set records for humidity and general unpleasantness.

"Why couldn't he just skip the pomp and circumstance, like any normal kid?" I asked myself as I headed for the freeway, yawning. "Why couldn't I skip the pomp and circumstance, like any normal nuclear mother? Coffee . . . that's what I need . . . "

With these thoughts and the sure knowledge that I was committed to hear a dull speech after a dreary ride, I pulled into the first McDonald's I saw. The coffee was essential, and fast. Maybe McDonald's was the catalyst. I don't know. I do know I began to remember bits and pieces of my son's life, one of which was that he couldn't eat anything, except hamburgers, french fries, Coke for the first 12 years of his life. Other memories of the early Charlie kept popping into and out of my head as I hit the road again, sipping coffee from a paper cup with the cruise control set and the fog on the road and in my head gradually lifting.

There was kindergarten. Chuck and Jim, the mirror-image twins. The neighbors called them the brothers or the twins because nobody could ever keep them straight. Their grandparents were constantly mixing up the names. Even Ed and I had trouble occasionally.

Suzanne, their older sister (by a scant year), always knew the difference, however. I remember her on the boys' first day of school walking between them, babbling and giggling, telling them to hurry up or they would miss the bus. Telling them not to suck their thumb, which was firm advice diametrically opposed to that which she usually gave them when they were troubled. Her usual counsel was, "Suck your thumb. Feel your blanket. You'll be OK." Now she told them school was different. Don't suck your thumb! The boys nodded solemnly.

"Oh, God, they're all so little," I thought, watching through the front window.

Then that image was gone. A jumble of impressions followed. I remembered Charlie climbing the little elm tree in our backyard when he was four, and swinging the tree top back and forth like some enormous feather fan. "I'm a bird! I'm a bird!" he yelled. I remembered teeth chipped by baseballs and hockey pucks, assorted stitches endured to repair assorted cuts and scrapes. There was the concussion when he fell out of his top bunk bed and the other one, worse, when he slid down the ski hill riding a piece of heavy plastic and collided with a tree. Who knows what close calls there were on that dumb mini-bike? I don't want to know.

Little League triumphs and defeats, the day camp he hated, the family vacations he loved, his awful coronet lessons, his first serious romance, and his second, how ponderously he pondered his responsibilities as part boy and part man — I remembered all these things and much more in tiny segments with no continuity.

I thought of all the other cars coming from other directions and bringing other family members to witness this intrinsically dull ceremony involving other children. I knew all of those strangers must have minds full of this same jumble of emotion and memory which I carry. Theirs was for somebody else; that could be the only difference.

I parked the car and found Jim. I sat with him and Chuck's special friend, Susie, high up in the crowded auditorium, and we cheered for Charles Edward McWhirter as his name was called and he walked across the stage in that silly robe and cap to accept his academic reward. We applauded the speakers, and later we took pictures and hugged each other, and then had lunch in a little local restaurant. Chuck and Jim were full of "do you remember the time . . ." conversation, and there was lots of laughter.

Then I knew what commencement was all about. I knew why I had driven through the heat and fog and was so full of joy for having done it. The speeches never matter; the ingathering does. All my routines and normal concerns had stopped on that muggy Saturday. It was Charlie's day, and just driving there and being there forced me to spend it in remembrance and admiration of him for the past, present and future. Quite apart from his academic accomplishments, I spent that day realizing once more how closely our lives are interwoven and reaffirming the mini-miracle of family and blood.

I'm very glad Charlie wanted to take part in his own commencement ceremony and even more glad I decided to set that alarm. Jim wonders if I would like to come to his commencement next year. I wouldn't miss it.

— June 13, 1979

All want a second shot at planning a wedding

Emily Post, in her wisdom and long before her dotage, decreed all weddings of American princesses are to be planned and supervised by their mothers. This is because no woman is ever completely satisfied with her own wedding. She wants a second shot.

Planning a daughter's wedding provides that opportunity, and at the same time, it assures the daughter will be at least mildly dissatisfied and, therefore, eager to plan a wedding for the succeeding generation. There is usually sweet reason behind venerable custom.

I am about ready to prepare my final, Mother of the Bride prenuptial report on the impending wedding of Suzanne Ford McWhirter and her intended, Michael Robert Orlicki, of the Livonia Orlickis. Nobody in either family will read it, since we are all approaching the throw-up stage concerning this American social event of the decade. I can be candid. In order to provide support for other mothers and their daughters, I feel I must prepare the Wedding Chronicles. Those who do not remember the past are condemned to relive it, according to George Santayana, who probably wasn't thinking about weddings at the time, but you never can tell with philosophers.

July 2, 1979 — At a downtown restaurant over a quiet lunch with her mother, Suzanne suggests that she and Mike are thinking about perhaps considering the remote possibility of seriously pondering the prospect of marriage at some vague time in the distant future. "What do you think about that?" she wonders. "Swell," I say, adding, "please pass the pickles."

July 9, 1979 — Suzanne telephones to say she and Mike are engaged. They would like to be married before the end of the year. "Holy cow!" say I, cleverly. Suzanne sighs. "I have known him for five years," she reminds me. "Besides, when I told you we might consider marriage you said, 'Swell.' " "That was just a few days ago!" I remind her. "We considered it," she says.

Remainder of July — Set wedding date. Change wedding date three times, driving the church secretary green beans. Plan budgets.

Tear up budgets. Replan budgets.

August to present — I forget what happened. There were the contracts with the club, musicians, baker, photographer, florist, engraver of invitations. There were all those dresses to find and agree upon and purchase. There were parties and dinners and luncheons. It's still going on, and I haven't been so excited or had so much fun since my Uncle Duke took me bush-flying in his Piper Cub. There is the identical feeling in my belly, too.

Through all of this glorious madness, I have discerned some universal truths which might be valuable to others. They include:

• The mother of the bride should buy a beige dress and keep her mouth shut concerning the details of its construction. It would only sound awful in the telling and cause all other female members of the family to moan, "Ooooooohh . . . and you've already had it ALTERED!"

• The mother of the groom should buy any color dress she pleases but observe the same silence rule for the same reason.

• The grandmothers of both bride and groom should buy any dress of any color and style they like, tell everybody who asks all about it, and be prepared to hear all the female members of the family gush, "AAhhhhh . . . that sounds lovely." Grandmothers can do no evil in the minds of children, grandchildren, aunts and female cousins. Fathers, grandfathers, uncles and male cousins would just as soon not be bothered hearing the details of feminine dress since they are pre-occupied with the details of male dress — those funny dinner jackets with the pleated shirts and the patent leather shoes.

• Making budgets is a waste of time because everything except the paper napkins will cost more than planned. There will not be enough paper napkins.

• No matter how thoroughly and carefully you think you have planned this wedding there will be a half-dozen things you have forgotten to do or have done in some sloppy fashion. This will reinforce the bride's resolve to plan her own daughter's wedding someday, and do it right!

• Your daughter, if you are lucky, will ask to spend the night before her wedding alone with you, at home, talking quietly about the warm, wiggly past and the shining, uncertain but surely adventuresome future. That's what Suzanne and I have planned. That, and probably popping some popcorn.

— Nov. 21, 1979

Weddings are to cry for
— and usually after, too

"When are you going to write about your daughter's wedding?" asks a stranger in an elevator. I am always startled to be recognized by strangers who know something. Then I remember I blab a lot about what's going on in my life.

"I thought everybody had heard enough," say I. "It was just a wedding." Just a wedding! Bite your tongue, Nickie.

"My husband and I have been waiting and waiting. You can't tell everybody there is going to be a wedding and then not tell us about it."

Oh, yes I can. I smile and get off on the fifth floor. Later I take an office poll and check my mail. It's wedding 6-1.

How shall I do this? I could write one of those little three-paragraph wedding announcements I used to write when I was learning newspapering.

"Suzanne Ford McWhirter became the bride of Michael Robert Orlicki in a double-ring candlelight ceremony at the Congregational Church of Birmingham on Saturday, Dec. 1 . . . " She looked beautiful.

I'm not saying it because she's my daughter. Maybe a little. Mostly it was because earlier in the day we had gone to see Dennis the Devastating at the Greenhouse. He had curled and clucked over her hair so that it was all shimmery and soft and very pretty. Then Anna dabbed a little makeup here and there on Sue's normally soap-scrubbed face. Sue wasn't sure she liked it.

"It looks great." I said. "You don't know what you like."

We hit the car and the freeway, heading for the church. Sue pondered her face in a mirror and wiped off the lipstick. She replaced it with no-color lip gloss.

We met the bridesmaids at a hotel suite near the church. They curled their hair and giggled. They blushed their cheeks and drank champagne and talked about school days together, old boyfriends, new husbands and whether their dresses were going to fit. Their dresses fit.

" . . . The bride wore a dress of ivory satin and Alencon lace with a chapel train. Her Juliet cap and long veil of illusion were trimmed with the same lace. She carried a bouquet of white camellias and holly leaves . . . ”

There were a zillion tiny buttons on those dress sleeves. It took two people 15 minutes to button them as Sue stood like a quivering statue. “Does the veil look OK, Mom? It doesn't look tacky, does it?”

“It looks lovely,” I said, and it did. Sue had made the veil herself and had stayed up until midnight the previous evening stitching lace appliques and thinking about whatever brides think about.

We did not have the popcorn on wedding's eve. We had a late supper instead. We talked about when Sue was a baby and I bathed her in a mixing bowl because she amounted to only 4½ pounds of bones and yowling mouth. We talked about her growing up. I gave her the “something old,” which had been her great-grandmother's, and we both got teary.

“ . . . The mother of the bride wore a long gown of champagne-color dull satin and chiffon, trimmed in gold bugle beads and tiny sequins. The mother of the groom wore a flowing chiffon gown of pale mauve . . . ” You bet we did. Fade into the woodwork, that's us. I worried about the sequins, but they were OK.

“ . . . A reception, dinner and dancing at the Bloomfield Open Hunt Club followed the ceremony.”

It was jolly, and lasted until 2 a.m. I forgot to put out a guest book which I had remembered to buy. The bride and groom forgot they were to dance the first dance, so I did, with Larry DeVine. The bride and groom forgot they were to change clothes and leave at a decent hour so polite folks, who wouldn't dream of leaving before the bridal couple, could leave at a decent hour. People left when they felt like it, which was late. The bride and groom were the last ones out. I forgot to toss the confetti and rice which I had put in a Baggie and stuffed in my purse for the occasion.

On Monday evening following the nuptials, my telephone rang. “Mom?” said Suzanne. She sounded quiet and tentative.

“Are you OK, sweetheart?” I asked. “Is he a beast? Are you coming home?” She laughed. She said Mike was fine. Life was good.

“I just wondered if you were, well . . . a little down because the wedding is all over. I thought maybe you might need cheering up,” she said.

“Who, me? Are you crazy! I'm GLAD it's over. It was a lot of work. I'm fine!”

"OK," she said, bubbling again. "See you soon! 'By!'"

Goodby. I went upstairs to put something in a closet and ran smack into Sue's wedding dress, wrinkled now, a little dusty at the hem, with a tiny rip in one underskirt where her heel went through it during a whirligig dance with somebody. I looked at the veil she had made, and at the buttons on the sleeves. I cried.

— Dec. 12, 1979

I can take the altered state of one less son at Christmas

Charlie may go to California for Christmas. It's not for certain. He's thinking about it. I've been thinking about it, too.

Charlie is my son, also called Chuck. He's half the matched set of sterling twins I sometimes refer to as Price and Pride. Jim's the other half.

Charlie has some time off between jobs. He has some money saved. His father has recently moved from Illinois to California. Charlie says, "It would be good to see Dad again, and it would feel good to get some California sunshine. What do you think, Mom?"

Think? I think I hate the idea.

It would be the first time in 25 years, since the boys were born, that I have not been with them and their sister on Christmas Day. It would mean one less plate and chair at the dinner table. It would mean one less voice in the living room. It would mean sitting around opening gifts without Chuck and Jim laughing together, poking each other and making their ritualistic, customary jokes about how Mom always liked one son better than the other. It would be terrible!

I'll think some more. Maybe it's OK.

California sunshine would certainly be pleasant. And Ed would certainly enjoy spending Christmas with his son. He'd like showing Charlie around the new house and town, playing tennis with him and opening presents with him on Christmas morning.

He would get just as misty-eyed as I've been known to get on Christmas morning, sitting around in a robe, drinking orange juice, nibbling warm rolls and talking with this grown-up son. They would admire the tree together and, from the corner of his eye, Ed would admire Charlie and feel such pride in him. I know the father pretty well.

Ed would look beyond the branches of whatever passes for a Christmas tree out there in Lala Land. He would see other trees, a succession of green spruces and pines. There would be the shimmering mirage of long abandoned electric trains, hockey sticks and skates, baseballs and bats, sleds for belly flopping. There would be puzzles and picture books, a red dump truck, a brown bicycle. Ed would see all the surprises and clutter of 25 Christmases that delighted this young man, starting when? — about two weeks ago, when he was a little boy. Ed would consider the Christmas visit a wonderful gift, which it would be.

What the heck. Chuck going to California for Christmas is no big deal. He isn't flying off to Rio with the Rolling Stones. He's going to feel sunshine and see his father. He's going to share himself for a little while with someone he loves, who loves him back. That's a good thing.

It may be emotional vitamins for me, too, and for Jim, Sue and Mike, Sue's husband, who seems to have joined the close society of McWhirter kids and become as much one as if he had been born to it.

Nothing human is forever. No rituals or relationships endure unchanged, unaltered, untouched by the passage of time. Love does not hinge on place or time. Love does not depend for its strength and endurance upon sameness, the same people together, doing the same things, compulsively, year after trudging year.

Tradition and a ritualistic coming together can unite a scattered family. Coming together at the same place on the same day each year can be a comfort to people who are loose in the world, drifting or struggling against a current. Going home to the place where the tree has always stood and the table has always been set, where the faces are predictable and welcoming may represent a kind of security in a world of dread and danger. It isn't essential, however. It isn't even important if everyone is secure and unafraid of abandonment to demons.

Charlie's thinking about a California Christmas is a healthy reminder to his mom and other moms that a child is neither property nor chattel . . . that love does not bind, but liberates . . . that being apart from a loved one is never abandonment, but just an altered state. I hope he gets one of those el cheapo flights and remembers to make it round-trip.

— Dec. 7, 1981

A mother's serious illness provokes fear and anger

Mother is in the hospital again. It's very difficult for me to concentrate on anything else.

I mean, I was just going to sit down and write something flip and cheerful — the fancier the stationery, the weirder the letter was one idea, although I'm not sure the premise holds. Anyway, I gave up on that because Mother is in the hospital again.

There is a strange mix of emotions which course through the human psyche when someone close and much loved is very ill. There is anxiety and a sense of powerlessness. There is fear and hope. And there is anger. Anger is the strange part.

I remember being very angry on several occasions when some especially loved person was ill. It was more than anger. A couple of times it could only be described as rage.

The object of the anger was never the sick person, or any person at all. It wasn't even anything as vague as bum luck, fate, providence or God. The anger was general and unfocused.

How outrageous that this fine human being should be suffering! How stupid that this person should be in a hospital bed instead of out soaring among the stars. How wasteful, illogical, purposeless, random and wrong. Wrong, wrong, wrong! That's the kind of anger it was, and is.

What's wrong with somebody getting sick? Nothing. Everybody gets sick from time to time. Eventually everybody wears out and breaks down, piece by part. After 40 it's just patch, patch, patch. (I read that on a birthday card once and have chuckled about it ever since.)

I think the sense of outrage has to do with myself. Friends, people I love, certainly my children, perhaps especially my mother, are all part of me. I am angry because a part of myself is suffering and ill. I am offended and diminished by this illness which afflicts an integral part of my own larger body. I rage against it.

Is everything selfish? I suppose so. I know that when one grieves for the dead it is rarely grief for some loss to family, society or humankind. It is very subjective sorrow for self. What have I lost?

What comfort, love, humor, joy or inspiration must I now do without? Of what pleasure am I now deprived?

The more personal and pleasant the association with the afflicted person, the more personal and unpleasant the response to the affliction. We are not objective or rational about any of it, and rage may be as appropriate an emotion as sorrow or fear.

Beyond this, mothers represent something special in everybody's life. It doesn't matter if one's mother is loved or despised or holds some emotional rank in between. For her child, Mom validates and perpetuates childhood. As long as a mother lives, her child remains a child.

What I know is that a mother's death emotionally marks the absolute, irrevocable end of childhood for each of her children. One doesn't assume the total regalia and credential of adulthood as long as Mother lives and one must assume that credential upon her death. It is a second puberty, a maturation not to be further denied or postponed.

So to rage against the illness of a mother is to rage against the potential loss of one's own childhood. It makes no difference whether the child is 16 or 70. The sense of it is nonsense. The emotional reality is rock hard and palpable. Mother and I will talk of these things during our next visit.

— March 23, 1981

The spirit sags a moment, then life's demands nudge

Nickie McWhirter will return this week. I know that because I read it in the newspaper.

If I hadn't read it, Nickie McWhirter probably would be sitting at her dining room table poring over notes and scraps of paper with unfathomable messages scrawled in her mother's hand, quite uncertain in the last few months.

She would be sorting through folders containing old photographs, yellowed letters, cards, newspaper clippings, birth announcements and death notices concerning four generations-removed relatives whom she does not recognize and never knew.

She would be staring at stacks of china nut cups and bone plates, wondering where in reason's name to store these things, since the idea of parting with them is unthinkable; wondering, too, at the size of ancient cupboards and the ancient families which had routine use for these items.

If I hadn't read in the newspaper where I would be this week, I would be awash and drowning in 75 years of my mother's memories and my own heritage.

Mom died last week, after a long struggle. She was in the hospital more than she was out of it during the last two months. Her mind was sharp and her spirit was unintimidated to the moment of her death. Her body had been exhausted for some time, however. If it had not been for the still-vital neurons and dendrites whipping reluctant parts into daily action, I doubt Mom would have made it beyond springtime. She was iffy as long ago as last Christmas.

On the day of her death — wired to a heart monitor and with assorted other machines assisting her own built-in and failing life-support system — she talked optimistically of the future. She definitely would get better. When she was better, she would move into a supervised residence of some sort. She would not listen to any talk about nursing care, because all she needed was a little help now and then, " . . . some people to keep an eye on me."

In the middle of just such a quiet conversation, her heart quit. It would not be coaxed by hospital personnel with all their skill, chemicals and machinery into resuming its labor. Some of the nurses wept.

I tell you this because it is still prominent in my thoughts and because some of you, who knew my mother slightly through my writings, will want to know. And, I'll tell you something else, which is important.

It is good to have work to do.

I used to wonder at the silliness of funerals. I used to think they were burdensome and barbaric. I used to think the parents and children and other relatives of persons who died ought not to be expected to arrange funerals and then greet other relatives and friends and go through the ritual farewells. I used to figure it would be better if somebody else took care of all that and left the family alone with their sorrow. I was mistaken.

There is nothing to do when you are alone with sorrow except remember good times and not so good times and wish you could relive some of each, which is impossible. There is nothing to do at all, except let some of your own spirit sag and seep down cracks.

The work, for which human beings are all designed, quite properly intrudes and insists. It includes planning a funeral, right now, and no excuses. It includes being present to greet people, accept their love and love them back. The work affirms life and living. The work absolutely demands life, at the same time it respectfully acknowledges death.

Then, if you are as lucky as I, there is other insistent work to be done. There is a job that demands its share of attention and energy, and extends its share of love and sympathetic understanding.

I keep remembering a line from a T.S. Eliot poem: "Hurry up, please; it's time. Hurry up, please; it's time." It echoes through the memory of my mother lying in her hospital bed. It whispers in my own ear as I am tempted to linger over the memories of her lifetime, strewn on my dining room table. Hurry up, please. Nickie McWhirter will return this week. Hurry up, please. It's time.

— Oct. 21, 1981

Discovery on a closet shelf dusts off a fond memory

After my mother's death came the physical and emotional work of sorting, saving, discarding and reorganizing her things. Among them I found my father's diary. It was in a stack of dusty books stored on a closet shelf.

Dad died more than 20 years ago. I had not forgotten him, but I had not thought about him much recently either, until I found the diary.

Dad read books, listened to music, fixed broken things and worked in his bacteriology laboratory. He liked learning about everything, from new poets to astrophysics. He called it discovering.

He shared discoveries. Unlike some fathers, mine enjoyed kid questions and would always put down a book to answer. How can the grass freeze and die in winter and come back to life again in the summer? What is the Milky Way? Why don't people just keep growing and growing until they are taller than houses? He never gave silly or perfunctory answers.

Dad used to ask me as many questions as I asked him, leading me with him, step by step, so I could personally discover the answers I was looking for. It was like solving a puzzle. It was fun. He said it was better to learn this way. Things you discovered belong to you forever. Knowledge that is handed out pre-packaged and perfect is easily forgotten, he said. Besides, the information could be wrong, or incomplete. It might be misinterpreted.

"Try never to take things on faith alone," he told me. "Question and test everything you can."

Dad's philosophy sometimes got him in trouble with preachers. Preachers annoyed him anyway. He thought most of them were pompous. He didn't think any preacher knew it all, or even half of it, or ever could. He mistrusted the infallibility of the Bible and saw no blasphemy in that skepticism. He mistrusted all totalitarianism and authoritarianism. He said Christ did too, but the preachers had conveniently forgotten that part.

My father's life had a center, but it was not himself or mother or me. It was not his work and certainly not the organized church as he knew it. It was his God, however.

It was a presence which, like the enormity and complexity of the universe, my father could not see clearly, touch or fully comprehend. He knew it was all there, however, and that he was a part of it, which fit perfectly. It was the Creator and the Creation, taken altogether, in awe of which my father stood, like a delighted and wondering child, all his life.

Despite his admonition to me to accept nothing on faith alone, he accepted everything on faith. It was his own faith that the universe made perfect, if sometimes incomprehensible, sense of. The sense was not found full and ripe in books or human pronouncements, however. Much of it was waiting to be discovered, bit by unlikely bit. Observe, question, hypothesize, experiment, learn, grow.

I was reminded of all this because of the diary. It encompassed entries made during the last year of my father's life, which began with him healthy and ended with his death from cancer. Interspersed with meticulous notes about his laboratory projects, accounts of gatherings of friends and trips with Mom is his growing awareness that ominous changes were taking place inside his body. Then there is the shocking diagnosis and prognosis. Finally, there is his continuing to live out his days as usual, as long and as fully as possible.

The last entries were made shortly before he lapsed into a coma, from which he never emerged. They had to do with the weather, visitors, old friends, new ideas being kicked around his sick bed. There is nothing at all about pain, fear, apprehension or self-pity. In a near final entry, he noted, "The adventure continues . . . "

Until I stumbled on this diary, I had forgotten my father's enormous, unshakable, but nameless faith. I had forgotten his courage. I had forgotten his gentleness. I had forgotten how much I owe him as a teacher. "The adventure continues . . . " and I am still learning at his knee.

— Nov. 22, 1981

People with clout
are not sweetie or dear

"Can I help you with something, dear?" he wonders. Dear! I am standing in an aisle of a hardware store. All I want is an extension cord. I have no desire for an intimate relationship with this nerd of a salesman who is a stranger to me.

"I need an extension cord, with a switch," I tell him, trying not to snarl. He smiles.

"Right over there, dear," he says, pointing. Dear, indeed! I'm going to punch him out! No, I'm not; I don't know how. I'll give him a one-two with words. I'll tell him he can call me ma'am or madam or miss or Ms. or even Mrs., but he damn well better lay off the "dear" stuff! I'm not dear to him and he's doing nothing to endear himself to me.

"Thank you," is what I tell him.

"Sure, dear," he says. Aaaarrrgh! I pay for the extension cord and exit, steaming.

Driving home, I am still furious, as much with myself as with him. "If you never tell a jerk he's a jerk, he'll never know," I say to me. "Yeah, but even if I told him he wouldn't understand."

Maybe. I wish I had told him, anyway, I should have, just for the exercise. I should have said . . .

. . . Pardon me, sir, but please do not call me or any other woman with whom you are not well acquainted such things as honey, sweetie, babe, baby or dear. These endearments and any others of your choosing are appropriate forms of address only to women with whom you have a personal, affectionate relationship, and then only if the woman or women find the terms acceptable.

You see, when you call me "dear," you presume and imply things. You presume that I would be flattered or pleased to have you as an intimate. That's quite a presumption and quite unlikely. You imply that we already have some special relationship which permits you to call me cutesy-poo names. That's false.

Most important, by failing to use the title miss, Mrs., Ms., madam or ma'am, you fail to recognize me as a fully functioning adult person, female-type. You put me in a box with all the other possible "dears" in the world. These include puppies, kittens, gentle dumb-bells of either sex, baby orangutans and most small children. The box ought to be labeled "assorted Anonymous Weaklings." They are all nameless, impotent little dears.

Perhaps it would help you to think about the selectivity with which you use these terms, instead of respectful and appropriate titles. I suspect that you call women whom you do not know by name "dear" only when you consider the women servile, powerless or inferior. You might address a waitress or a child or maybe an old woman as "dear." How about a female police officer? — as in, "But, dear, I was only going 50 miles an hour." How about a doctor? "The pain is right here, in my chest, dear." I don't think you would do that.

People with clout are not sweetie or dear. People with clout are sir or ma'am. All men are sir, by the way — unless they are little boys. Then they are young men. Little girls are never young women. They are little ladies or young ladies or sweethearts. Phooey.

It is the parallelism you need to keep in mind. If you approach a man in the store, how would you address him? Maybe you say, "Can I help you?" (You should ask, "May I help you?" but we aren't going to be graded on grammar today.) You may add the "sir," but maybe not. At any rate, you don't say, "Can I help you, lover?" If you did, you would get either that punch I didn't throw or an improper proposal, neither of which is what you had in mind. Probably.

In short, you would not presume or imply with a man what your adorable little "dear" presumes and implies with a woman. So cut it out. And tell all your friends to cut it out, too. You know the ones: The hotshots who call nurses, librarians, clerks, receptionists and all secretaries "honey." It's OK to write letters to female columnists and begin them, "sweetheart." Don't try it on the phone, however.

— *Dec. 13, 1978*

We must refuse to build any new stereotypes

As recently as a half-generation ago, the working mother of small children needed to be able to defend herself from her neighbors. It was not that anyone stoned the house or spray-painted, "Mother, Stay Home!" on the garage door. It was just that the majority of American moms did stay home if they possibly could.

Unless there was pressing economic need, a mother who chose to work outside her home was considered a very strange fish. Everybody wanted to know why she behaved so peculiarly. Hardly an explanation sufficed. I know about this because I was one of those strange fish.

The minority position has become the majority position sometime during the past decade, however. Today a woman with skills or education who does not have some gainful employment, at least part-time, is the one likely to be considered oddball. Friends and neighbors want to know how she can possibly be content to stay home raising babies when she might also be working her way up through some corporate organizational chart.

Hasn't she heard of the trapped-housewife syndrome? How about the empty-nest syndrome? Maybe she's just lazy or weak, intimidated by her husband.

Surely she understands the insurance tables which suggest she's a cinch to be widowed long before she's ready for perpetual care herself. And there are those other ominous statistics which show that one marriage in three now ends in divorce, with alimony fast becoming an historic curiosity.

A woman who does not prepare herself for financial independence and self-sufficiency at the same time she is preparing baby formula is a fool, according to contemporary philosophy. Her survival may depend on her ability to earn a paycheck and her self-esteem will suffer if she never tries.

At the very least, this argument goes, wives and mothers should get involved in organized volunteer work which imitates the marketplace. The training and discipline will be useful; the contacts will help on that inevitable day when these women decide they want or need full-time employment.

Most of that is true, I believe. It is a realistic and pragmatic view of the feminine condition.

Recently, however, a young wife and mother who lives in a cushy suburb complained about this activist-woman lifestyle and reminded me of a responsibility many job- and career-focused women may have forgotten, me included.

"It's getting so a woman feels guilty or lazy if she chooses to stay at home and take care of her house, husband and children," she said. "It's worse than that. We feel stupid. It's as if everybody else thinks we're just too dumb to hold a job. I really resent that. It isn't fair."

If the strange fish have taken over the pond, they/we are evidently no more tolerant of alternative lifestyles than the old carp who used to dominate. That's embarrassing.

In the beginning, circa 1965, what the feminists wanted and lobbied for was choice. Women should have all the choices available to men. Women should not be funneled and cast into stereotyped roles. Women should be free to choose from all available alternatives without guilt, fear or ostracism. Go, go, go . . . win, win, win!

The winnings have been enormous, thanks to a lot of help from friends, primarily in the federal government. There is still much to be won, but the concept that a working wife and mother is healthy and admirable was an early trophy. We have come to love it and consider it something every woman ought to have in her personal collection of values.

That's as oppressive an idea as the one which says every woman ought to be thankful she's married and a mother and doesn't work at anything except homemaking and child-rearing. Maybe we haven't been paying attention.

If it is guiltless choice and smashed stereotypes we want, we must respect all choices and refuse to build new stereotypes of women to replace the old. The new woman who is a corporate vice-president at the same time she is the mother of four has no more intrinsic value than a childless woman or a woman with one or 10 children who stays home and cares for the brood.

We have got to stop defining human value according to jobs and life patterns and start defining it some other way. Is this person kind and giving.? Is she contributing to society and people close to her? I don't know exactly which measuring stick to use, but it is clear that women have pretty much won the right to work for pay or not, depending upon personal circumstances, and still be respectable. I hate to think the women who work will castigate those who do not and just flip the token over from where it was in 1965. That is not progress.

— Nov. 16, 1979

A frightening lunch
with the Stepford Wives

I had lunch last week with three of the Stepford wives. They drove down from a mid-Michigan city I won't name. These three have not yet been processed and they are reasonably sure they will escape robotization, but life is iffy where they live. I told them I would do what I could to help. At this distance, however, and with no voice in the Stepford Men's Club (it's called by a company name up there) I don't honestly know if I can be very effective. Pray for us.

These three women are all under 35, I judge, and any one of them could play Mom in a Hostess Twinkie commercial. They are all college graduates and upper middle-class. Their husbands are either directly or indirectly involved in the Men's Club.

I shouldn't say husbands. One of the wives is divorced. The reason, says she, is that her husband was disappointed. He wanted someone who would stay home, bake chocolate chip cookies, attend fashion shows, plan dinner parties for the husband's business associates and otherwise be supportive of the Club view of what men and women and marriage are all about. She could do this, she noted, and did — with one eye shut and only six neurons synapsing. That was the trouble. She was restless. She told her husband so and got a job. He told her she was a trouble-making malcontent. They split. He found himself a no-brainer female who thinks baking chocolate chip cookies, on demand, is what God intended women to do. His boss is pleased.

Stepford is an idyllic place, you may remember. Men run it and their women are robots, programmed to please the men in every way and be content doing so. Stepford wives love to iron and scrub and cook. They are beautiful and they adore their husbands. They are totally subservient. They never question masculine judgment, caprice, authority or ineptness. The Men's Club has its standards, which prevail. Strangers and non-Club members are unwelcome.

I found "The Stepford Wives" — book and film — an interesting Gothic tale, frightening in its extension of the Playboy fantasy into marriage and beyond. It portrays the complete dehumanizing of women — their obliteration. In the tale they are replaced by machines, which appear human and lovely, but are incapable of thought, emotion or any behavior other than that built-in and programmed by their husbands.

What intelligent, healthy man would want to live with such sterility, such non-challenge, such un-surprise? I didn't think any, until I met the women from the Upland city. They assured me that the most admired women in their town come close to Stepford wives. The trouble, my companions say, is living and loving in a setting dominated by a single, strong company. The company becomes the Men's Club; the husbands are comfortable in the Club and the Club leadership expects certain behavior from the wives — subservient and dedicated to traditional values.

"You know what we are going to do after lunch?" asked Wife No. 1.

Nope.

"We're going to find a movie theater that's showing 'An Unmarried Woman.' We want to see it and it won't come to our town."

How does she know? She called the film distributor and he said so. No explanation.

I'm shocked. This is a current film with fine reviews.

"That's nothing," she says. "We didn't get to see 'Julia' either. Same reason. The company disapproves."

"An Unmarried Woman" deals with a wife who is dumped by her husband and finds that, although the going is rough, it isn't all that bad. "Julia" is about two women friends who are serious, strong, effective human beings. It is anti-Fascist and anti-authoritarian. "Julia" was an Academy Award nominated film and one of its stars, Vanessa Redgrave, won the award for best supporting actress. How much power must a company — a Men's Club — have to keep such a film out of a community? More than I can imagine.

"We have a club, too," says Wife No. 2. "We call it the Mystery Club. It's all women, wives." What do these club members do? She giggles.

"We meet once a month and the hostess plans a mystery trip. It is ALWAYS something to do out of town. The whole idea is to get away. We keep it secret, the place we're going. We don't even tell our husbands."

That way, see, no husband can criticize the activity and tell his wife that maybe the boss wouldn't approve. These devil-may-care females do such zany things as visit the Detroit Institute of Arts, or maybe attend an out-of-town movie, or lecture, which has been quietly and unofficially banned back home.

You guys out there are going to think I made all this up. I didn't. I guarantee it is true, and happening in the state of Michigan, as told to me by three rational and well-educated females, who live with it. According to them, most of the other Stepford wives consider these three peculiar and dangerous. Their own husbands are some uneasy about the rebellious attitude they display — not wanting to stay home and bake chocolate chip cookies. All of this frightens me, and I don't know what to do about it.

— May 15, 1978

This business trip becomes another soap opera episode

It sounds like an episode of "Dallas" or "As the World Turns." It is instead, the remembered experience of a Detroit woman and it concerns sexual harassment.

Ellen had recently been promoted to a middle-management executive position in a large corporation. She was the first woman to hold this job — praise hard work and federally scrutinized affirmative action programs. Like many such women, she did not lack ability, but she was a little short on the self-confidence which comes with experience.

Daniel was a co-worker. He had been with the company only a couple of years but had been promoted twice and was considered a man on his way to a top job. He was good at his work and confident to the rough edge of arrogance.

Dan and Ellen were associates on the job and equals on the corporate organizational chart. So much for the cast of characters.

The action began some time ago when these two were assigned to travel together to New York City for a day of meetings, conferences and assorted other business chores. Dan and Ellen arrived at their New York hotel, briefcases in hand, the evening before their business appointments. They were shown to separate rooms and met later for dinner.

There were a couple of cocktails and some talk about the business to be conducted the next day. Dinner was pleasant in a dim, candlelit dining room. Dan ordered wine. He touched her hand. He complimented her on her appearance. Ellen was increasingly aware that Dan was behaving like a courting male and this made her uncomfortable.

Finally and fairly early, Ellen asked to be excused. She said she was tired from the trip and wanted to go to sleep. She reminded Dan that their first meeting was scheduled for 8 a.m. He agreed and they headed for the hotel elevators.

Dan opened Ellen's hotel room door for her, using her key which he eagerly snatched from her hand. He walked in. She thanked him and suggested he walk out again. "I'll see you in the coffee shop for breakfast at 7," she said. Dan smiled.

"Let's order a nightcap," he said. "You are really uptight!"

Ellen told Dan as plainly as she could that she had no interest in anything but sleep — which she intended to do alone, right now. She told him to leave. He told her not to be a "bitch." He loosened his tie, took off his shoes and flopped down on her bed, smiling. Ellen was furious.

What followed was a ridiculous playlet in which he lurched and grabbed, she shoved and pushed. He tried to maneuver her to the bed and she tried to get him out the door.

"It sounds silly now," she says, "but at the time I was scared. He was stronger. He bruised my arms. I was afraid to scream at him for fear someone would call the hotel security people. I didn't want to hit him. I think I was afraid he would hit me back. I would be damned if I would cry or plead with him! I felt totally intimidated and powerless. It was a terrible experience and it was silly at the same time. I kept thinking it wasn't really happening. It was like a dream or a scene from a cheap movie."

Ultimately our heroine managed to shove her momentarily off-balance co-worker out into the corridor and throw his shoes after him. She bolted and chained her door. She fell into bed.

Ellen went to breakfast the next morning still shaken and uncertain what her course of action, if any, should be.

Dan arrived for breakfast looking refreshed and rested. He complained of a hangover, however, which seemed odd since Ellen knew they had drunk comparatively little the night before.

"I hope I was not an embarrassment last night," he said. "I probably shouldn't drink. You know, I can't remember anything after we had dinner. Not a thing! It was probably that wine you wanted." There was a warning in that nonsense which was telegraphed to Ellen instantly.

She thought, "You SOB. The wine was your idea. And we were both perfectly sober."

Ellen assured Dan, icily, that he had done nothing unacceptable. "Good," he said. "That must have been some wine! Anyway, I'm glad I didn't misbehave."

He was lying and she was letting him. She had some premonition, however, that if she complained about his behavior or reported it to their mutual boss, Dan would lie with equal ease to protect himself and discredit her. She was a corporate experiment and everybody knew it. He was already tagged for corporate success.

Ellen could imagine Dan telling the boss that Ellen was the one who went a little crazy on this first big expense account trip out of town. She drank too much. She got her snoot full and misinterpreted his concern and kindness for a pass. Of course, he took her to her room and saw her safely inside. Good thing, too. She could hardly walk!

Ellen knew that Dan was capable of convincing lies. She was unsure if she could make the truth sound plausible. She didn't want a fight she couldn't win.

Ellen decided to do as Dan was doing and pretend nothing unusual had happened. Hell, she HAD kicked him out. She won, didn't she?

The sight of Dan made her skin crawl after that, however, and it still does. These two no longer work together but circumstance occasionally tosses them into the same room at the same time. When this happens, Dan smiles at Ellen as if they are dear friends who share some intimate secret. They do.

He raped her emotionally, if not physically, and she let him get away with it. She knows that by not complaining, not even to him, she tacitly approved of his behavior and made herself a partner in her own humiliation. His gratitude is galling.

The incident was more than a cloddish pass, rebuffed and forgotten. It was a skirmish in some dominant/submissive battle. Dan won. Ellen lost by default. That's how sexual harassment usually works and why it is doubly reprehensible.

— *Feb. 17, 1980*

There's still a need to heed Friedan's 1963 message

In 1963 I sat at a kitchen table reading Betty Friedan's book, "Feminine Mystique." It was about 3 p.m. one afternoon in mud season.

You remember seemingly unimportant details about seemingly unimportant days once their importance is fully understood. This was one of those days.

I was in the kitchen because I had been cooking and because I planned to greet the kids at the back door as soon as they hit it from the school bus stop. I would tell them to take off the muddy boots right there.

So, I sat for perhaps only 20 quiet minutes reading Friedan and significantly reprogramming my life, although I didn't realize that part until sometime later.

Friedan's book, for those unfamiliar with it, is now credited with marking the beginning of the modern feminist movement. It is a gentle work by later standards. It attempts to explain away the myths of what it is to be masculine or feminine in our culture. It points out that many traditional and prized feminine roles amount to learned subservience to male dominance. It suggests many valued feminine qualities are actually symptoms of capitulation to oppression.

I remember reading one part in which Friedan notes that male children are always asked what they will be when they grow up and are always expected to say they will be doctors or firemen or some such. That they will father children and play that role is taken for granted. Female children, however, are expected to respond that they want to grow up to be mothers and wives. That they might want jobs or careers as well is considered bizarre. Or, it was so considered in 1963.

About the time I read that part of Friedan's work, my own tads came squealing and sloshing towards the back door. I slammed the book shut to save the recent scrub-and-wax-job on the floor. In the hubbub of boot removal, I asked some questions:

"What do you think you'll want to be when you grow up?"

After the inevitable giggling, punching and poking of each other, my boy twins, sometimes called Flotsam and Jetsam, pondered their mysterious futures.

Jetsam said, maybe he'd invent cars for some auto company. He was just beginning his continuing love affair with the internal combustion engine. Flotsam didn't know. "Carry a briefcase and go to work every day at the office like Dad" was as far into his future as he could see. Neither boy mentioned marriage or babies.

Suzanne thought the whole question was dumb. Pressed, however, she decided she would get married, live in a big house and have four babies. I cringed.

"But what will you do?" I asked.

She frowned. "Make cookies and stuff."

"No, no, darling," I said. "I mean, will you have a job besides?"

Puzzlement decorated her face. "Maybe a teacher," she said. "Maybe a nurse like Aunt Barbara." And she was off to change into her mud clothes and go outside.

That was when I knew Friedan was right. I learned a lot of things in an instant that late afternoon 18 years ago.

For one thing, I knew I had to get a job. My kids, especially my daughter, needed a much larger pool of female role models. The best and easiest place to start was with myself. I was employed full time, newspapering, within a year and have never stopped.

I mention this for two reasons.

The first is to remind everyone of both genders of the importance of role models and that there still aren't enough diverse female models in most of our lives.

Children of both sexes learn much of what it is to be a man or a woman from the men and women around them. When we deprive kids of the experience of knowing women who are carpenters and doctors and corporate vice-presidents, we deprive them of valuable knowledge. They need it to figure out who and what they are or will be and how they will happily relate to others, including a spouse and children should Providence provide.

It is not always possible to fill a household with family members and friends who are women carpenters, doctors or vice-presidents. It is always possible, however, to fill a household with the idea that these women exist and these possibilities exist. And it is certainly possible to expect the school system to lend a hand in this idea formation.

Which brings me to the second reason I remembered that long ago day in mud season and decided to mention it.

I was appalled recently to find that in at least one elementary school class in Birmingham, Mich. — a supposedly enlightened community — children were being asked to list careers suitable for males and females.

With encouragement from the teacher in this class, boys were listing such careers as doctor, lawyer, race car driver and football pro. Girls were being encouraged to list nurse, teacher, ballet dancer and housewife.

One girl child did think about being an auto mechanic and put that on her list of female careers. The teacher suggested she remove it. The teacher thought auto mechanic an unrealistic and inappropriate choice for a female.

May the ghost of Susan B. Anthony haunt that teacher. And may the rest of us who care about giving all kids the widest possible choices in their lives keep a sharp eye on the school bus. There is a lot worse stuff that kids can track into the house than mud.

— *Jan. 11, 1981*

Economics has upper hand in the battle of the ERA

Once more the Equal Rights Amendment has suffered a temporary rebuff. Once more the central issue of legally acknowledging women as self-determining citizens, assured of all the rights, privileges and protections, as well as the responsibilities, of full citizenship could not be embraced by two-thirds of the largely male U.S. House of Representatives. Once more the familiar rationalizations for opposing the ERA were presented.

The genuine reason for opposition is still abundantly clear, however, and in all of its abject ugliness.

Economics is the core. The ERA, if ratified, would bring into question many laws and legally permitted business practices presently in effect which discriminate economically against women. Rectifying inequities would cost billions of dollars.

There are some states, for example, in which estate tax laws permit a man to inherit his wife's property and assets without penalty. The same laws extract considerable estate tax against property and assets inherited by widows. Since women generally outlive their husbands, such states stand to lose considerable revenue through equal treatment of widows and widowers.

In states without no-fault divorce laws, a woman who fails to follow her husband to a different residence is usually considered guilty of desertion, a ground for divorce. A man who fails to follow his wife is blameless. Again, the wife is guilty of desertion. The deserter rarely is rewarded with a generous settlement.

Such state laws rely on vaguely moralized justifications. The true function of such laws, if not their announced purpose, is to perpetuate female dependency and preserve an existing power base. The power is money. The base is firmly held by men.

Such laws and practices would certainly be challenged and would probably be toppled should the ERA be ratified. In addition to tax and divorce laws, unequal disbursements of Social Security and other government benefits, insurance benefits, school supplements and other legislated disbursements would need rectifying. The cost to persons, institutions and government presently profiting from the traditional economic oppression of women would be substantial.

Conventional morality is the shield frequently raised to justify economic immorality. It obscures our view of what is really objectionable to the profiting and powerful. What is truly objectionable is sharing the wealth equally with that half of the population which is currently legally handicapped.

It is my belief, firmly held, that the various emotional arguments raised against ratification of the ERA are diversions meant to hide this genuine, economic inequity which is addressed and redressed by the amendment.

Despite high-sounding moral argument and Bible thumping, I believe leaders of the anti-abortion opposition to the ERA are at least equally concerned with keeping women economically dependent (read it barefoot, pregnant and out of the mainstream of economic life) as they are concerned with the welfare of unborn children. Ditto those who would protect us from the imaginary bugaboos of homosexual marriage and women in combat, a couple of moralistic haunts conjured to scare us from looking at dollars and cents.

Note I said leaders of the opposition use these ploys. Many of the foot soldiers are true believers that morality can and should be legislated — despite all historical evidence to the contrary.

Equal self-determination and privilege under the law regardless of sex is the ERA's promise. In return, it demands both men and women relinquish any existing, special, sex-linked privileges. Women have much to gain and almost nothing to lose. Men have a great deal to lose. It's largely money. That's what the argument is about, and why it has raged for 60 years. The prize is, obviously, well worth going after. Persevere.

— *Nov. 18, 1983*

Do Harold a favor, let him do the wash

He had a paperback book in hand, the title of which was something like "The Peasant Gourmet." Anyway, I asked about it and he said he expected the book to make his life, henceforth, considerably more pleasant.

"Our parents do a terrible job teaching us how to live," he said. The "us" meant men in the unmarried state. He's one. "I'm sick of hamburgers and pizza and frozen food. I don't understand all that cookbook stuff about browning and sauteing. This is going to be great!"

This — the cookbook — appeared to be a collection of pot recipes. Throw it all in a pot and ignore it for three or four hours. Some of the stuff sounded strange. Pineapple, coconut and shrimp, with a few other additions, was one entry. Anyway, this guy of about 30 years had decided to launch his early education in the domestic arts. I wished him luck and told him to stick with it even when the going got rocky. Souffles, and cleaning the carpet, for example.

He has a valid gripe that parents do a bum job teaching boy children how to live independent adult lives without mom or a wifely substitute handy. The situation is improving, but not much and not fast.

A generation ago the Army, Navy and Marine Corps must have taught legions of males how to sew on a button, iron a shirt and wash their socks. I know gyrenes were taught to make beds. Most of them conveniently forgot all the lessons on discharge day. I don't now know more than a couple of men over age 40 who are comfortable in the presence of an ironing board. Most of them contemplate the board and its companion steam iron with loathing, as if they were some exotic instruments of torture.

Ed McWhirter, miffed at a drawer full of folded, perma-press handkerchiefs, once bellowed, "What does a man have to do around this house to get an ironed handkerchief?" I think that's when the marriage began to quiver. I suggested, "A man might iron one." He didn't respond positively. I ironed. That's how it was in the covered-wagon days.

The idea that our then seven-year-old daughter was routinely ironing handkerchiefs, table napkins and assorted other flat stuff just for fun, and never burning a finger or finding it terribly complicated, didn't suggest to him that he could do it, fearlessly. Men do not iron. QED. Too late for him and those of like mind. It's not too late for their kids and grandkids.

By the time Sue and her brothers were in high school, the boys demanded ironing lessons — shirts, slacks, assorted other essentials in their bopper wardrobes. They didn't consider ironing infra dig, just a useful skill. A generation of progress, though slow.

Now there are some middle and upper schools which teach courses in bachelor survival to boys and young men. How to sew on a coat button; how to scramble eggs and toss a salad; how to sort laundry and combine it with the proper powders and potions to turn out clean clothes. That's a start, but not enough.

Unless young men get a chance to practice these things routinely at home, they forget — just as their dads and granddads forgot everything domestic our military tax dollars taught them. By the time the adorables get to be 25 or 30 and are ensconced in their bachelor quarters, they are hardly better equipped to cope than the previous crop.

It's a pathetic thing to see an upwardly mobile young executive, a future captain of commerce and industry, pile a supermarket cart full of Stouffer's frozen lasagna. It's embarrassing to hear him sweet talking a female neighbor into doing his laundry in return for moving her piano. That's OK once, but laundry needs doing several times a year, at least. Pianos aren't moved that often.

So, it would seem reasonable that pre- and immediately post-pubescent males be given every opportunity while still in the bosom of their families to learn what they need to know in order to survive and prevail over their soon-to-come bachelor state. A sharing of the regular daily or weekly or monthly rituals of cooking, housecleaning, sewing, laundry wrestling, bed-making and the whole mishmash on an asexual basis might do it. If boys and girls learn to work the lawn mower and snow-blower and family car on an equal basis, why not the range, the steam iron and the vacuum cleaner (including attachments)? The latter machines are simpler.

Finally, in making this pitch for early masculine domestic training, moms, dads and children of America ought to consider this:

Very few of us of either sex need to learn to change a tire. It is a potentially useful skill for all males and females, of course. There are few times, however, when any of us must change a tire or want to — what with road service and telephones. And tires don't go blewy that often in the course of a normal, prudent lifetime.

Buttons pop constantly, however. Stitches disintegrate, opening seams in jackets and hems in trousers and skirts. We eat two or three times every day. Our homes are our living environments, and if they are grungy, we feel grungy.

Each of us needs to know how to take care of these basic domestic needs quickly, efficiently and pleasantly in order to be whole, happy adults. Raising a gang of human beings who have been deprived of what they need to know in order to live independently is a cruelty. It keeps males in bondage to mom or wife, dependent children — until they swallow the false pride they were taught at home and decide to learn for themselves what they should have been taught easily as kids. A cookbook is a good start.

— Feb. 6, 1978

The limits of masculinity might include painted nails

We were at a party, and most of us were barefooted. That sometimes happens at summer parties. Shoes come off, and people sit around wiggling their toes in the grass. It feels good.

Someone noted the men's toenails looked quite plain compared with the sparkle and slick of the women's enameled toenails. So we decided to paint the men's toenails.

Some of the men laughed and co-operated in this zaniness. Others firmly declined the paint and were content to observe and shake their heads in mock disbelief.

The men who shunned painted toenails couldn't say why, or didn't say why. The men who submitted to painting didn't say why either — except to note some curiosity concerning how male toes might look with painted red nails.

The experiment in silliness ended soon after it began. A bottle of nail polish remover and cotton balls were produced. Before they went home the men were all restored to their unembellished state, more or less.

The most interesting thing about the toenail painting episode was the strong emotional jolt it seemed to produce in the men. Those who opted for no paint were adamant in their refusal. Even the most co-operative of the twinkle toes was obviously not completely at ease until the paint had been removed.

It was as if painting male toenails were scandalous and somehow made the men vulnerable to charges of being less than fully male and heterosexual. I thought that was pretty funny. How could 10 dollops of paint threaten anybody's sexual identity?

We have certainly placed narrow limits on masculinity in our culture. Men can't cry, of course. We all know that. They can't display confusion, indecision, sorrow, fear or weakness. Displays of love or affection are discouraged except when focused on worthy women (who decides the worthiness?) and then such displays are to be made privately. No ruffles or frills are allowed in male clothing. And men certainly can't paint their toenails.

Women get to wear almost any style of clothing in any color we choose. We can paint our nails, we can paint our faces. Women are also allowed to weep, giggle, be afraid, hug, kiss in public and become confused whenever we become confused.

We don't have to do any or all of the above, but we are allowed. Our gender is not discounted for such behavior. Our sexuality is not threatened.

That's a kind of liberation which many women take for granted and which is rarely mentioned. When it is, women sometimes complain that they are expected to exercise all these options and more, whether they feel like it or not. The entire package is what society and especially men have come to regard as "feminine." Another time we can discuss whether that makes any sense.

What is important here is that men are so unliberated in terms of emotional and personal presentation. Their package of masculinity is tiny and harsh. Mostly it contains prohibitions, things labeled "thou shalt not." There are a few mandatory and painfully inflexible "thou shalts." Men have few choices and options. They are kept tightly bound in formal tradition and stereotype. I'm not sure all men even understand their predicament.

If women cherish the freedom to express emotions openly and present themselves imaginatively, I think we have an obligation to the other half of our species to share that freedom. We need to encourage men to expand their view of what is masculine and appropriate. By experiencing more on all levels, men will come to know women better and be less afraid of us. Men and women will be able to love each other more, and better.

I have never met a man who regularly painted his toenails, but if I ever do, I don't think I will mind. Pink is out, however.

— July 15, 1981

Sure, men know everything about women — just ask one

Most men don't know much about women, and what they think they know is frequently mistaken.

What they think they know derives primarily from their unfledged youth and the experiences of early conquest. This initial skirmishing is usually accomplished by the time a male is 25 years old when, in the American tradition, these boy-men marry. They settle unwittingly into intellectual and emotional stagnation on the very subject which has obsessed and compelled them for the preceding 10 years, and probably will for the rest of their lives: Who and what are women, and what do they want from men?

That such men have not mastered even their elementary lessons, let alone progressed to advanced or post-graduate study, rarely occurs to them. That their laboratory exercises have utilized girls, rather than women, as partners frequently goes unrecognized or else it is simply discounted as irrelevant. That what they think they know about woman has mostly to do with sex, and how to get it, never seems to suggest a certain shallowness of concept.

When some self-doubt or mature curiosity concerning the essential female emerges — perhaps during the fabled mid-life crisis years — most men are likely to put the idea of personal ignorance aside.

I am told it is common for the mid-life male to reassure himself of his masculinity and his understanding of the female personality with obvious facts. Chief among these is the fact of having had a wife and kept her well, inside or outside a pumpkin shell.

It is widely assumed by many men, for example, that if a man has remained married for a number of years, he probably has demonstrated he is sexually competent and smart enough to have figured out how to keep at least one woman happy. What is happy? Happy enough not to leave him for a life with the mailman, or a life alone. That's the minimum requirement. If he can keep one woman happy, this reasoning goes, he must surely understand womanliness including its foibles and eccentricities. Women. They're all alike!

If the wife has borne children and obviously enjoys them, if she is family-centered and nurturing, this is all the more proof that the husband is female-wise and competent. After all, it was and is he who made possible her familial pleasure, dear girl that she is.

If more proof that the adult male knows how to make women happy is required, almost any man can call up from memory his secret collection of remembered one-night stands and short- or long-term affairs. In retrospect, these are taken as irrefutable proof of a man's virility, attractiveness and capacity to please.

Didn't the blond from Cincinnati say the sex was very good, and didn't she make him promise to call her again if he ever came through town? Wasn't Marilyn at the office wonderful — wanting marriage with him all those years, but understanding when he explained he could not abandon a wife and three children?

Surely such a man understands women very well!

Why, then, do so many women laugh at such a man? Married, single, old, young, contemporary and traditional — the women laugh. Read the magazines; see the movies; listen attentively to lunch-table conversation or ask any woman you know and trust to be truthful. At first they only laughed quietly and to themselves. Increasingly, they are laughing in public and in front of the men.

A man who thinks like the one described above, which is the majority of males, knows very little about women; that's the funny part. He knows only what he knew at 17 or 27, at best. He considers women to be stagnated and frozen in womanliness exactly as they were when he was learning about them, or thought he was.

Because, in his arrested awareness, he is still a child, albeit inside a man's body, he continues to expect women to play childish roles. He expects them to persist in the child-women stereotypes which were never fully valid and which women have long since outgrown or abandoned. These are primarily sexual stereotypes because men apparently see women almost exclusively in sexual terms. (How odd, when women see men as much more than genitalia in search of satisfaction. No matter.)

Sometimes he likes women to play Mom. She's the one who cooks, clucks, nurtures and cares. She is practical and forgiving. She has little interest in sex, but great interest in his comfort. She smilingly waves "hello" and "goodby" and makes sure the socks in his suitcase match each other and his suit, and he hasn't forgotten his briefcase.

Sometime he wants a woman who will be the innocent Girl Next Door. She trusts and accepts. She is uncritical and unsullied. She considers him a hero, and because of her innocence, she has no other heroes for comparison. She wants none. This pleases him very much, and uncomplicates his life.

Every once in a while he wants a woman to be the Naughty Girl Down the Block, the one who will come across in the back seat of the car on the first date and never tell, or ask for anything better. She is "dirty" and, therefore, lucky to have any attention paid her at all. She should be grateful. She is exciting and good for sport, but nothing a man need take seriously.

Wives and mothers, mistresses and one-night-stands are all expected to fill some, all or combinations of these blatantly sexual stereotypes and in so doing demonstrate womanliness a man can understand and manage. It is no awesome wonder that whole women are amused by the simplicity.

All women are all of the above, and much more. They are minds and voices, spirits and substance. They are high achievers wearing bodies which can reproduce life itself. They are sexual, but more than sex, and many, perhaps most of them, are moving out in all directions at once with very high energy and expectations. They are male-threatening on many conscious and subconscious levels.

Because women are more than men ever imagined or chose to investigate in our lifetime (never mind the long generations earlier) and because each individual woman has continued to grow from what the men in her life thought they had all figured out at age 17 or 29 or 46, women tend to scare men to death. If women would just stand still! But they can't and won't and are not meant to.

When divorce occurs, as it does now once in every three marriages, women do more than scare men. They terrify them.

It is time for remedial gender lessons. My dad called them bonehead sessions. The bookstores, libraries and newsstands are full of what men need to study and learn. (Women have been doing their book learning about men for years.) Our bedrooms, living rooms and kitchens are available laboratories. The women are everywhere, and most are quite ready to co-operate in some greater or lesser experience of male enlightenment.

This is what feminism is about and why it promises human, not just "female," liberation. I was going to tell you this good news on Susan B. Anthony's birthday, but I didn't have a column that day. Please don't say: "Just like a woman."

— *Feb. 25, 1980*

Right to one's own body extends even to supercops

I understand Frank Serpico, New York's supercop, is an unwed father. After reviewing some fancy medical testimony, a Manhattan family court recently found Serpico to be "clearly and convincingly" the father of an 18-month-old baby boy. The mother is identified only as Pamela P., an airline flight attendant.

Pamela P. took Serpico to court to ask that he be ordered to pay child support. Having found that Serpico is the father, the court is still iffy about support.

Serpico has a feminist attorney, Karen DeCrow, a former president of the National Organization for Women. She argued that her client was tricked. He had no intention of impregnating Pamela P. and fathering her child. Sex, yes. Love, commitment, marriage or fatherhood, no. He apparently made all this very clear, very early in his short, cozy relationship with Pamela P.

According to testimony, Serpico asked Pamela P. before the first of several tussles in the sheets if she were using a contraceptive. She assured him she was. She was not.

In court, DeCrow contended Pamela P. willfully set out to entrap Serpico and make him the father of her child. Serpico said he felt he had been victimized and used as a "sperm bank."

He never expressed and still expresses no loving interest in either the woman or the child. His position is cold and decidedly ungallant, but it's consistent.

After pondering all this, a woman judge, Nanette Dembitz, ruled in Serpico's favor. Although he is unquestionably the father and got to be so in the usual way, the judge said he will not be ordered to pay support for his son if the mother can assume the financial burden herself.

"Petitioner's wrong," said Dembitz, "precludes her transfer to him (Serpico) of her financial burden for the child she alone chose to bear."

The judge is now trying to decide if Pamela P. can afford the cost of her folly, or heart's desire, or whatever the baby represents. If so, she's welcome to it. If not, Serpico may yet be ordered to cough up some of the dough he presumably has squirreled away, from the movie which bears his name.

Meanwhile, the judge's ruling and the feminist lawyer's so far successful arguments have raised a tempest among other feminists. How can we allow a man to use a woman sexually and lustfully (Serpico has not denied this part), father a child and then abdicate all responsibility for the child with the excuse that he didn't mean to become a father and was given no choice? Outrageous! Or, is it?

What DeCrow did was use a basic feminist position, upheld by the Supreme Court in its rulings permitting abortion and the easy dissemination of birth control means, as a defense for a man.

If a woman has a right to her body, a man has a right to his, she said. If it is OK for a woman to decide when and with whom she has babies, quite apart from when and with whom she has sex, a man deserves the same right. If it is wrong for a man to impregnate a woman against her will, it is equally wrong for a woman to use a man's sperm for her own impregnation against the man's will. If a woman can choose not to bear an unwanted child, a man should be able to choose not to assume paternal responsibility for an unwanted child.

The issue is still sticky and the judge's ruling is potentially revolutionary to family law. I vote with the bench and Serpico, however. Sexual entrapment in any of its forms by either sex is despicable. It certainly sounds as if Pamela P. knowingly made herself into a not-so-tender trap.

If women want all the sexual freedoms formerly reserved for males in our society, we are going to have to give up the special sexual protections formerly reserved for us. We can't demand the exclusive right to our bodies and then use pregnancy to trap men into marriage or support payments. The right implies responsibility, which we will have to assume. Serpico may be a creep, but he appears to have played honest creep in this sad scenario.

— Nov. 15, 1981

If sex is the problem, is silence the answer?

A friend, whom I'll call Louise, has been complaining recently about her live-in boyfriend, whom I'll call Sam.

These two are about 30 and finished their sexual internships long, long ago. They have been in private practice together — his place or hers — for about four years.

There is trouble in Paradise, however.

As close as I can figure out, Sam isn't interested anymore in those magic moments. A hug and a snuggle and a good-night kiss are about as much as Louise can count on with any regularity. Sometimes she's lucky to get that.

"Have you two talked about it?" I wonder.

"I tried a couple of times," says Louise. "He made some lame excuses and then he got mad. I don't mention it anymore. I've found something on the side."

The something is a married man, 44, who wants to stay married. He has the same problem with his wife that Louise has with Sam. It all works out.

Louise says her exercise companion has ducked talking to his wife about his dissatisfactions. "He doesn't want a hassle and, anyway, he's happy now."

No he's not. Neither is Louise. Sam certainly isn't happy, and if that nameless, faceless wife out there is happy I'm the Princess Caroline.

What they all are is bored and frustrated and feeling guilty about it.

One of the strangest phenomena in man-woman relationships is that the more we care about someone, the harder it is to talk to that person about what's really bothering us. If the bother is sexual, it's nearly impossible.

We talk to our housemates candidly about politics, hemorrhoids, budgets, vacations, pre-menstrual tension and whether or not beef fondue is one of our favorite things. Only sex is off limits. The good stuff is supposed to happen magically. We learned that in the movies.

We remind each other to hang up the coats and stop putting wet towels in the laundry hamper. But we choke down any urge to say, "I'm turned off by this routine. Let's try something new. You tell me what feels good and I'll tell you."

They didn't write lines like that for the movies until recently.

There is something threatening to both partners when either expresses sexual dissatisfaction.

What's wrong? Is it that I can't respond or that he can't perform? What's wrong? She always liked this before and now she obviously doesn't. Maybe she doesn't love me. Let's don't talk about it because I can't stand to hear any "yes" answers.

The trouble is our parents taught us that sex is sort of good, but sort of dirty and nothing to discuss over dinner at Grandma's house, let alone with strangers.

So, we all learn our routines early and privately — somewhere between puberty and about age 25, with strangers. We don't talk.

We get locked in.

We get married, either officially and legally or unofficially and without benefits of license. No more fooling around. This is IT.

We go on in the same old way until the libido languishes and unfocused resentments turn waspish and off, completely.

Then, we blame the person we're living with for being dull, boring and insensitive. The complaint is returned, with interest.

Some people settle for living this way the rest of their lives. Maybe Sam has.

Others, like Louise, take to looking around, individually and secretly, for that something on the side, or a succession of them.

Neither alternative is satisfactory in our society which preaches monogamy out of one side of its mouth and, out of the other, tells us we are entitled to super sex as long as we both shall live.

Sex counselors say that the thing bored sex partners should do is start talking openly with each other and then laugh, play and experiment a little until they again find something exciting, rewarding and mutually satisfying.

But don't expect miracles

I think that a certain amount of boredom in sex is inevitable and natural. It should be expected, if not enjoyed. There is no way to sustain or substitute for the mystery and excitement of discovery which are part of the new sexual encounter.

I wish it weren't true. I wish people could get married and live happily ever after, growing ever closer and more loving, bringing their bodies and minds into ever finer harmony and all the rest of that good stuff we thought was possible from what we heard in church and in the movies.

It doesn't work that way. I don't think human beings are cut out for monogamy. I think we are as naturally polygamous as alley cats. That goes for both sexes.

Unfortunately for us, it is neither practical, legal nor morally acceptable for us to live that way.

So the trick to making monogamous sex work as well as it can is to try all those things advocated by the Drs. Shearer and others from the very beginning — talk, play, experiment and conduct a mutual school of lifelong learning. But know from the beginning, too, that certain compromises will be made.

Sex with a tried and true partner, can be of Olympian quality and still be boring, at least temporarily.

The day will come when the sight of him sitting by the fire and puffing his pipe won't turn her on at all, but the milkman will.

The night will come when the sight of her undressing for bed will be as exciting to him as prune whip compared to the thought of the new secretary at the office.

It will be impossible to re-create the romance and excitement of the wooing and winning, no matter what the women's magazines say.

It will be time for the alley cats to prowl, or settle in for a little safe, human boredom. It's never an easy decision.

Happy Valentine's Day.

— Feb. 14, 1977

Displaying everything anybody wants to know

She is seated at a small table to the side and up near the music, up near the corner of the room where a guitar player perches on a stool under a baby spot, noodling and plucking out "Michelle" and "Send in the Clowns."

"If that doesn't say it all!" says my male companion. "Look at her. She has everything figured out."

I look. She is pretty, maybe 35, dressed in an ivory crushed satin tunic affair with black skinny pants and strappy spike heels. The attire is appropriate.

This is a Friday night in a suburban watering spot which has become a meeting and mixing place for the 30-and-up monied, unmarried or fooling-around crowd. It is snobby and expensive. The women all have attention-getting gimmicks. Glitter, spangles, feather boas, cocktail hats and plunging necklines abound. My friend and I have come to watch contemporary mating behavior. We are reminded of Beverly Hills and the Polo Lounge. At least, I am. It's fun.

This woman is not the prettiest or most dramatically attired female in the crowd, but she has the best sense of theater and she is employing it.

She sits close enough to the guitarist to share some of his light, making her face and cleavage much more visible than those of the dozens of other women in the room. Nice trick, but most amateurs know it. It says, "Look at me."

Like everyone else, she shares a table. Unlike everyone else, however, her partner is not a man or another woman. Across the table from Madame du Mystere sits an appealing girl child, perhaps 10 years old. This fairly screams, "Hey, look at us!"

No one brings kids to this place, not even for lunch. There is no reason not to and there is no rule against it. It's just very expensive and usually full of adults. On Friday night everybody is romancing, or cruising. Isn't a child a turnoff?

My friend and I observe. The child is demurely well-dressed. She is well-mannered. She chats happily with the woman. She seems comfortable in this environment, sipping her concoction of pop plus orange slices. The woman sips a Manhattan, on the rocks. The obvious inference is that these two are mother and daughter and that they are out on the town together, enjoying it very much.

"That woman won't be alone very long," says friend. I glance around the room. There are already at least a half-dozen pair of male eyes fixed on this duo. It would take Cheryl Tiegs in a bikini walking a chimpanzee on a leash to distract them.

"Would you look at that!" says friend. "Look what she's doing now. Wow!"

Wow? She is smoking a cigar. She holds a medium-sized, lighted cigar in her left hand — the one which does not wear any wedding ring. She seems comfortable with the cigar; she seems to enjoy it as if it were a familiar and quite unremarkable pleasure.

"Well, that cuts it," says friend. "I have never seen such a complete display of everything anybody wants to know."

By now a man has approached her table. They chat. Daughter is introduced. She chats. Man summons waitress and orders a round of drinks including more soda pop for Daughter. There is much friendly chatter and Man offers Madam a calling card. She accepts with a smile. He scribbles what we guess is her telephone number on the back of another card and slips it into his pocket. So long, goodby, lovely conversation. Man departs.

We watch this same scenario repeated with slight variations a couple of times. We leave.

"What's this 'everything anybody wants to know' business?" I ask my friend.

"A man always wants to know if a woman he has just met is married or single, if she has any kids, are they monsters or OK, stuff like that."

"And she just answered all those questions with this demonstration," I say. Right. She demonstrated a lot of things.

I think about them. She telegraphed that she was not looking for someone to go home with or take home with her. She had the child. There is no sexual pressure on these men, not tonight. But, she was also saying, "Come introduce yourself. We'll see what happens."

"What about the cigar?" asks friend.

"I guess it says that she is self-confident. Maybe she is innovative and experimental. She isn't intimidated by social conventions. She is not a prude," I say. He smiles lustfully. I frown.

"Her house probably smells like a pool hall," I suggest. He keeps smiling.

"She's a hooker! She's broke and can't afford a sitter. She's looking for a rich husband! She runs a child rental agency and is drumming up customers!"

He just grins and sighs. "You had better not try that scene," he tells me. "Your kids are too old. All the singles will go for them."

"I could smoke a corncob pipe," I suggest.

— March 14, 1979

Many of today's women do indeed kiss and tell

"Do women tell you just everything?" asked the dapper Daniel sitting next to me at the cocktail supper.

"Most women today are extremely candid," I said ponderously. I like being ponderous at cocktail suppers. "If you ask a direct question, you are likely to get a reasonably honest and very direct answer, about almost . . . everything."

We both knew that "everything" meant sex. That's what troubled this man — that women might discuss the more or less intimate experiences of their lives with near strangers, especially (gasp!) newspaper writers. I agreed with him that this is a fairly new and peculiar phenomenon.

"Does it frighten you?" I wondered.

"It terrifies me!" he said, and offered to refill my glass.

I was not surprised to find, when he returned to our shared perch on the fireside couch, that the conversation topic quickly changed to food, fashion and whether we were in for a more or less cruel winter than usual. Talking about "everything," even in this impersonal way, evidently made this fellow twitch.

Too bad. There was a lot more which could have been said.

I could have told him, for example, that most women I know are still fiercely loyal to their mates. I have never known one who was loving and committed, either in marriage or some monogamous living arrangement, to poke fun at the sexual technique of her partner, for example. I have never heard such a woman play back, sigh for squeak, yesterday's bedroom scenario. And most women still have the good taste and sense not to brag about their one-night stands, naming names, detailing dialogue, fumbles and scores.

Quite honestly, however, I also would have had to report to this fellow that under certain circumstances many contemporary women do kiss and tell, and probably more women blab, more often and with less discretion and guilt than do men.

I don't know when this behavior became manifest in our society. I probably wasn't paying attention. I know that as recently as 10 years ago, women sometimes confided to their sisters or best friends (never their mothers) some details of their sexual encounters, inside or outside marriage. In front of casual acquaintances and (gasp!) newspaper writers, however, these women behaved as if sex were something of which they had little personal knowledge and in which they had no conversational interest whatsoever. This was called modesty or propriety. It was considered a fine feminine quality.

Sometimes between then and now, an amazing turnaround has taken place. Women of almost all ages presently discuss sex with friends and even casual acquaintances without so much as a blush. They may not toss their own personal experiences on the table for inspection, but they frequently speak in generalities about men, women and cozy getting-together. They exchange opinions about what feels good and what doesn't. They talk about foreplay and post-coital cuddles. They exchange information concerning the emotional crises of temporary impotence and premature ejaculation. And they do all this without guilt or modesty.

I don't know of any sociological studies which chronicle just why, when and how this attitudinal change took place. We can only guess.

My guess is that sex as legitimate discussion subject came out of the vault shortly after the majority of American women began using the pill or other low-risk birth control method and after the women's movement had convinced great gangs of women that sex could be and ought to be fun. When great-grandmother's idea that sex was slightly smutty or something to be endured rather than enjoyed was discarded, women began to talk. If sex is not dirty, is fun and is not dangerous (i.e. likely to cause an unwanted pregnancy), then it is certainly something we all need to understand better. Let's talk about it!

In the talking, woe is us, many women do name names. We should not. It is very impolite and emotionally cruel. I certainly can sympathize with my cocktail-party pal's discomfort imagining that all the details of masculine amorous adventures might be shared by total strangers. Men supposedly did this sort of thing for generations, however, and some women justify their candor on this ground.

I'm not at all sure that as many men kissed and told, or presently kiss and tell, as women presume. It is a contemporary fact, however, that many women do. Maybe I should keep this information to myself, but I think we all deserve to know what's going on.

— *Jan. 4, 1980*

We either tell too much
. . . or nothing at all

He sat in a big wing chair with a glass of bourbon and branch in his hand. He talked, interminably, alternately glancing at me and at the fire flickering from the grate. He talked about himself.

In the course of an hour and a half I learned about his education, his career progress and regress, his parents and grandparents, his economic and social theories, his food and drink preferences and his distaste for abstract expressionist art. This done, we went to dinner.

Over lamb chops, the monologue continued. He confided that he is considered pinch-penny by some colleagues but that he is actually a prudent money manager and has the stock portfolio and financial reserves to prove it. He dislikes golf and tennis, but enjoys sailing and owns an old but sturdy craft. I learned its history. He personally dislikes housework but cannot abide an untidy house so he has assigned various chores to his two semi-adult male children and does some himself, temporarily. He cannot decide if it is wise to hire a day worker or "see what happens."

"It has been very difficult for all of us to adjust since the divorce," he says with a sigh.

"I understand," I told him, and I did.

Good night, Nickie. Good night, Abercrombie. Maybe we could do this again soon. Perhaps. I'll call. Please do. Ta, ta, pip pip, and fare thee well!

Time passes and I sit over lunch with a woman friend. "Tell me about your date with that guy, what's his name? The new one," she says.

"Abercrombie," I say. "Men need dating lessons."

"Sex lessons, maybe. Dating, I didn't think so," she says. "What happened?"

"Terminal boredom set in after the first drink," I tell her. "He told me about himself, more than I needed to know. He took all the mystery away. He didn't let me discover anything. He laid it all out like an adult."

She seems puzzled. "He IS an adult," she notes. "What did you expect him to do?"

I ponder this. "I'm not sure," I tell her.

I expected to get to know him just a little bit better. I did not expect a cram course in his family history and philosophy. I expected some hints and glimpses into what makes him happy or sad. I did not expect a documentary in Panavision and Technicolor.

"I expected a date, that's all," I tell her. "What I got was a job interview. I wasn't sure whether he was the applicant or I was. Anyway, I kept expecting him to offer me a job cleaning his house or whip out a contract for me to sign. By the time it was over, I felt like I had been out with my father; I knew that much about this guy. I even knew that cabbage gives him indigestion. We weren't eating cabbage!"

My friend smiles. "They either tell you too much or nothing at all," says she, "not counting the lies, of course." Of course.

I go back to work thinking about what I might put into a dating refresher course for the adult American male who has been out of it for a while. Then I decide it isn't just men. "They either tell you too much or nothing at all, not counting the lies," goes for women, too.

I remember a man telling me once about some woman he had met and dated, briefly, who he said poured out the history of her miserable former marriage on the first date and invited him to her family reunion the next weekend. He ran. Smart fellow.

We forget something about dating from the time when we are pros, at maybe age 17-22, to the time when some of us are beginners again, circa age 40. I think it is that discovery part.

Most adults I know, in the throes, are so goal-oriented they miss the fun. The goals are usually sex and/or marriage. Sometimes they are sex and avoiding marriage. The date becomes a means to an end and the only discovery of importance is discovering how long and at what cost the goal can be achieved.

Dating among the younger pros is not this goal-directed and frantic. It is slower and more casual. Much of the fun of dating is in the process itself, the process of finding out about another person, gradually unraveling mysteries, discovery. The fun is in the growth, from acquaintance to friend, perhaps to lover and, maybe marriage partner. Kids rarely get ahead of themselves in this process, or lag behind in order to protect their precious privacy either. I don't know of one of them who would tell a person on a first date that cabbage gives him indigestion. Let us all be as loose, and wise.

— *Jan. 5, 1979*

Sure, he'll buy — if you lend him $10 till payday

Some people are just cheap. It has nothing to do with how much money they have in their pockets or bank accounts. It's an attitude.

There's this man, for example, who recently asked a woman I know to do a little chore for him in her hometown of Detroit which he could not accomplish from his digs in Atlanta. The job was not complicated. It required a chunk of time and a few bucks, however.

He wanted copies of some records on file in a local bureaucrat's bureau. The man told the woman he would be ever so grateful for her help and would, of course, reimburse her for any expense incurred.

The woman spent the necessary hours examining this public information and arranging to have copies mailed to the man who, incidentally, is a former romantic partner of hers. She sent along a friendly letter outlining her effort and expenditures.

So far, and by now a couple of months later, she knows the material arrived, but she has not received so much as a polite "thank you" note from this gentleman. There has been no repayment of her double-digit spending either.

"I should have expected," she says. "He borrowed $20 from me on our first date. I never got that back. Then there were all those delightful Dutch-treat dinners he was so fond of. And the time he invited me to meet him for a romantic weekend in New York, and I ended up paying not only for my own air fare but the entire hotel bill for both of us. Great guy!"

Cheap.

Women, I rush to concede, traditionally have been considered society's cheapskates. Such women are called gold diggers. They have expected their male friends and companions to pay all the bills, do them favors, shower them with gifts and expect nothing in return except affection and a smile.

Gold diggers, however, are usually quite transparent. Most men know from the first "Hi, Baby," when they are dealing with one and that the financial and energy burden will be the man's, until and unless the woman suggests otherwise.

Cheap men tend to be sneaky. They don't usually telegraph their shots. They imply benevolence and deliver disappointment. Some examples gleaned from women who wish to remain anonymous:

• The man who takes you window shopping at Cartier three weeks before Christmas. He wonders if any little bauble you see is pleasing to you. Later, you rush out to buy him $500 worth of cashmere and silk in guilty (but joyful) anticipation of the Cartier bauble which will be your gift under the tree. He likes the cashmere and silk. He gives you a bottle of cologne and a hug.

• The imaginative fellow who suggests cocktails at his place followed by dinner at "a quiet little east side restaurant." The cocktails turn out to be the dregs of a bottle of domestic sherry better relegated to the stock pot. The restaurant is Chinese and is having a weekly $2.25 special on chicken chow mein, which he orders for two. After dinner he suggests a nightcap, at your place.

• The good friend and perhaps lover who speaks ecstatically of the new play or review at the Posh Tosh theatre, suggesting he would adore seeing the show with you and actually intended to invite you but has been unable to get tickets. Perhaps with your "contacts" you could swing it. You swing it. After the show, he tells you how marvelous you are to buy the tickets, and as his part of the evening, he would like to buy you a hamburger and a beer, if you can loan him $10 until payday.

• The adorable who invites you to a party at his house, says his boss is coming plus some important clients and he hopes everything will go well. When you politely ask if there is anything you can do to help, you find yourself assigned the job of planning, shopping for and cooking all the food.

I have never been able to decide if cheapos know they are cheap. Maybe they consider themselves frugal or sensible or practical. Maybe they can't empathize with their victims and see no victimizing. It doesn't really matter. If it is unattractive for a woman to be a gold digger, it is equally ugly for a man to be a cheapskate. The amount of expendable money, energy, thought and interest is unimportant. It's the attitude. It reeks.

— *Dec. 10, 1979*

Why Dimples can't dump Norman the Creep

"You aren't going to believe who called me again last night," she sighs with a heavenward eye roll.

"Who?" say I. "Idi Amin? Billy Carter? The IRS?"

"No. No. That would be pleasant. It was Norman the Creep. Can you believe that? After all the times I've told him to get lost. He wanted to go out to dinner or a movie or something. I just couldn't believe it."

"I thought you had told him you were married and pregnant," I say.

"I told him I was very seriously involved with someone," she says. "Then I told him I was engaged to someone. Then I said the someone was a very jealous, very big, very nameless member of organized crime. I thought that was creative lying. Did it stop him? No. He keeps calling. He probably checks the marriage license listings. He's just the kind of creep who would do something like that. Can you imagine!"

I couldn't imagine. Norman the Creep has been given every reasonable chance to back off gracefully, without overt damage to his ego. He has declined all opportunities. He persists in his amorous cuckoo mating dance. My friend now contends Norman suffers damage to that part of the male brain which is supposed to understand women. I don't know. Norman may simply be the most thick-skinned, heavy-egoed, bulldog-tenacious man in town.

Norman met my friend, whom I shall call Dimples, about a year ago. For Norman it was lust at first sight. For Dimples it was definitely ho-hum.

He soon asked her to go sailing. She said she didn't like sailing much and had a congenital tendency to mal de mer. He said, "Oh, come on." It was a pretty day; other people would be on the boat; it was just for an hour or two on a sunny Saturday afternoon. She said, "OK."

"Ten hours later I was stuck in the crummy galley of that crummy boat making sandwiches for those crummy sailors who were all drunk and still sailing on toward the North Pole!" says Dimples. "I was sick and had bruises all over my shoulders and hips from banging into the cabinets. There was a storm batting us all over the lake. I wanted to jump ship and swim for it when we passed the boat club, and you know I'm a rotten swimmer!"

About 3 a.m. Norman deposited Dimples at her apartment, soggy, aching, exhausted and with a still-uncertain stomach. "Then, the creep wanted to come in for another drink — just what he needed — and some huggy-kissy. Can you imagine?"

Can-you-imagine is said about Norman all the time.

It was after this first date that Dimples decided to pitch her new suitor. Unfortunately, good manners and all that motherly advice about how everybody deserves a second chance clouded her judgment. Norman dialed her up again and wondered if she would like to see a movie.

"Well," says Dimples, "I knew I wouldn't get seasick at a movie." She agreed. He picked her up in a van with a fairly filthy, cluttered interior. "I should have known everything would go wrong," she says now, in retrospect.

It was cold, below zero Michigan winter weather. The heater didn't work. The movie house was two suburbs and half a city away. The gas gauge showed empty, but Dimples thought it was probably just broken, like the shocks and entire suspension system of the van. The van made it to the movie house, miraculously.

Coming home was iffy. Norman the Creep noted he was low on gas and also pointed out to Dimples that something like steam was seeping from the cooling system of this machine. "I knew I needed antifreeze," he mused. "Better look for a cheap gas station."

"Cheap, that's him," says Dimples. "Here we were running out of gas and freezing up and he's tooling around every all-night, do-it-yourself gas station looking for one that will sell him a dime's worth of anti-freeze. I am shivering and freezing and praying we don't break down. He's saying he has known for a week, for a week, that his van needed antifreeze. He forgot about it."

Dimples noted at one point in this odyssey that her apartment building was a mere three blocks away. She suggested she get out and walk. He suggested they could probably chug there in the van and then maybe she would like to cook them a little something to eat since it was too late now for dinner out. He might just stay the night and find a cheap gas station in the morning. She slammed the door in his face at her first, and only, opportunity.

None of this has cooled the ardor of Norman the Creep. There have been numberless phone calls, day and night, myriad suggestions of other delightful adventures he and Dimples might pursue. Dimples has told him those tales of heavy involvement, engagement and everything short of marriage. She has used the respected turnoffs which begin, "I'm sorry, Norman. Sunday is impossible. I have made other plans." She has escalated these all the way up to, "I'm sorry, Norman. Next week, next month and the remainder of the calendar year are impossible. I have made other plans." Nothing works. Norman persists.

"He's like zits," she says. "Just when you think you're cured, up pops a Norman. God is punishing me for having lustful thoughts about Robert Redford."

Perhaps. "Lies don't work; that's obvious," I tell her. "You are just going to have to tell him flat-out that he is unpleasant and you don't want to see him or talk with him again."

"Cruel, Nick." She says. "It's too cruel. Besides, he'll want to get together one more time just so I can tell him how rotten he is. He'll want me to cook dinner for him and he'll plan to spend the night so we can talk about this rottenness. He's determined. He's thick. Creeps never know they are creeps."

"Correct," I say. "So there is only one other solution. You have to get married."

"Who'd marry me?" she wails.

"Norman," I tell her. Dimples is not speaking to either of us.
— *April 15, 1979*

It doesn't take radar
to detect a Miss New York

Miss New York is a pain. Sometimes Miss New York lives in Tampa or Phoenix or just across town. She's still Miss New York — and a pain.

Miss New York is your boyfriend's other girlfriend, the one he never talks about and would probably deny if you brought it up, which you do not, because you are still uncertain about how much of a civil disorder you wish to cause.

Miss New York is her name because, when you try to visualize her, she always turns out to be Shelley Hack in a white satin Charlie suit, swirling into the Cafe Carlyle on the arm of your very own Mr. Wonderful. Sometimes she's Candice Bergen waiting in front of the Pierre for a cab, giggling in the rain, with your Mr. Wonderful holding her umbrella and nuzzling her neck. That's him, and that's Miss New York, the hussy.

I don't believe much in women's intuition. Men say we have it. We don't. What we have is a keen eye and a sharp ear and fine minds well practiced in a prior reasoning.

That's reasoning from seemingly meaningless bits and pieces, to the discovery of the whole, round, warty truth. It is deductive. It is the reasoning which discovered black holes in the cosmos, not because they are visible, but precisely because they are invisible. They appear to be nothing, nothing, nothing at all. Women and scientists know that nothing is never nothing at all.

It takes most women about 10 minutes to know when the men in their lives are secretly trysting with Miss New Yorks. The more a man tries to create nothing, nothing, nothing at all, the more clues a woman finds.

He sees you only on Tuesday, Thursday and Saturday nights, for example. It doesn't matter what you suggest, he is somehow always too tired or over his head in work at the office on Monday, Wednesday and Friday nights.

On these evenings he doesn't even call to say, "Hi, Babes," or "Good night, Sweetheart." If you call him, you get the answering machine or no answer at all. He says he was so tired he just unplugged his telephone. This certainly suggests some pesky, recurring scheduling problem: Miss New York!

If he travels in his work, it may be noted his activities during his trips to Des Moines, Atlanta and St. Louis are always well discussed upon his return. He hardly has anything at all to say about what he did in Walla Walla. Odd.

He often telephones you, at all hours, during his travels to those other cities, too. He never telephones from Walla Walla which changes his normal pattern of behavior: Miss New York!

Ahhh — the semi-weekend you have just spent together has been filled with joy and languorous passion. Yet, you note he has had one eye on the clock for the past couple of hours. Suddenly he jumps to his feet, exclaiming, "Oh, my. Look how late it is! Where did the time go?"

He explains he just must get to the paint store before it closes. Paint store? Then he must go immediately to his place, alone, in order to start painting the basement. Alone? The basement? In six weeks he has never once mentioned his basement or any interest in painting anything. He has mentioned hating to be alone, however. He especially hates being alone on Sunday afternoons. It is now 4:30 p.m. Sunday.

There is just the teensiest hint in all of this that whatever project he has in mind has nothing to do with paint or basements. It could have something to do with his expected arrival somewhere or the expected and now-imminent arrival at his manse of someone: Miss New York!

It could be argued, and may be so by some male readers, that all of the above represents vexing female suspiciousness. Worse than looking for lipstick traces and sniffing business suits for the lingering scent of Nuit d'Amour, a woman who assumes the existence of a Miss New York from no more substantial evidence than a man's suddenly wanting to buy some paint or not wanting to talk about a business trip — well, she's got to be crazy. Wrong.

She may be sad or amused. She is not crazy. Most women not married and not involved in a going-steady arrangement are perfectly willing to accept the existence of Miss New York. They won't like her, but they'll accept her. Interesting competition is inevitable and actually enhances an honest game of courtship.

The galling part is the Dumb Dora role women are supposed to play. Men who go in for this transparent subterfuge apparently believe the women in their lives really don't know what's going on. The same man who is attracted to and respects a woman for her intelligence, wit, experience and good sense (not to mention body) somehow expects she will suspend all adult brain function and not notice when he starts behaving like a little boy with frogs hidden in his pockets. Isn't that strange?

"For three months I have been trying to think of some way to tell Jim I know about Miss New York," says a woman friend of mine. "I don't care about her. I'm not even mad at him for seeing her. I just want him to know that I'm not stupid and that I haven't been unaware of his lapses or swallowed any of his explanations and excuses. I can't stand the idea of him walking around believing he has put something over on me. Can you think of any way to tell him I know what's going on, without starting an argument?"

I can't. Except, maybe she could cut this column out of the paper and send it to him. I would put it in a pretty box, along with a rose.

— June 2, 1980

People look for the friend who'll share even the bike

He is unmarried and lives with no one except himself. I reiterate that lifestyle. We were talking about stuff in general and ultimately got around to marriage, divorce and the increasingly popular practice of unmarried folks living together.

It was our observation that while we used merely to read about live-in lovers, now almost everybody we know is one, or was one, or is thinking about becoming one. He named several, and I named several. They are our friends, neighbors and co-workers.

Some of these alliances have persisted many years without legal marriage and seemingly without emotional distress. Sometimes the partners remain financially independent with "his" and "her" incomes, charge accounts and possessions. More often, however, the twosomes share bank and stock accounts, car loans and even home mortgages. The live-togethers move around from city to city in pursuit of happiness just like the legally-weds. And they remain in these quasi-married states, apparently contentedly, often for many years.

"Why is that?" says my conversation partner. "Why do people who love each other not want to get married?"

"I don't know," say I, in true puzzlement. "Maybe they're afraid they could end up in a divorce court being bled to death by lawyers and judges. If you choose a roommate and make a mistake, you can just walk away. Swearing, perhaps, taking or leaving behind more than is fair and reasonable, perhaps, but you can at least walk away and not spend the next several years of your life in court. Unless you are Lee Marvin."

He doesn't like it when I say disrespectful things about lawyers or judges because he is one of both. We generally disagree on all matters having to do with the usefulness of the courts. That's because I say outrageous things, and he takes them seriously. He chooses not to get into that battle again this time, however, and fixates on the unmarried live-ins again.

"I think people who live together but don't get married doom their own relationship," he says. "It's bound to fall apart for that lack of commitment."

"But they say they are committed," I tell him. "They always say that. They say they don't need a piece of paper to prove anything and that legal marriage is a form of bureaucratic bondage or something. I have also been told by these lovers they are afraid their perfect union will change and falter if it is not totally voluntary and unfettered."

He looks judicial. "Do you buy any of that?" he asks.

"Not much," say I. I tell him I agree that marriage changes relationships. That's a universal, crystal, pure truth. Whether the change is good or bad is hard to judge right away. It's hard to judge an egg until you cook it and eat it.

"What I mostly think," I tell him, "is that people who live together without being married are withholders. They may be loving, loyal and committed, as much as it is possible for them to commit, but they are still withholding some of themselves. Some of their freedom and future is socked away in a triple-locked private vault. It's like some kid saying to his best friend that he'll share all his toys except, of course, for the 10-speed and the fielder's mitt."

Later, I ask a woman who recently married her former, longtime, live-in partner what made them decide to marry and how their lives changed after the ceremony. I tell her I assume they just got more and more comfortable together and finally decided marriage was a good idea. She told me I was dead wrong.

"Our relationship was great in the beginning," she said. "The last two or three years it got worse and worse. I was grouchy. So was he. We were both sniping at each other most of the time. One day we sat down to talk about what was wrong and how we felt and what we could do about it. I suppose we might just as easily have ended it right there. We decided, instead, that we had too much time and energy invested to throw it away. We decided to get married."

That is not the romantic story I expected. "How are things now?" I wonder.

She smiles. "Great!" she says "I didn't know it at the time, but before we were married, I just couldn't make the same emotional investment in him. Time, concern — I couldn't really get into his life. There was a private part I couldn't intrude upon. I didn't have the right. I guess I held him off the same way." Now, she says, they are both relaxed. All the "keep out" signs are gone. So is the anger.

People come together more or less fully, as they feel safe and secure. Everybody is looking for a best friend, however. We call it different things as we get older, but it all comes down to best friend. Given enough time, I think everybody gives up on a withholder. It doesn't matter that the withholder is swell and lovable in every other way. No kid can ever be best friends for long with somebody who won't share it all, including the bike and the fielder's mitt.

— Feb. 15, 1980

Love is not easy,
no matter what the age

He calls her his "little dago," and in the peculiar way in which love purifies and transfigures all it touches, the ethnic slur on his lips becomes a term of affection and endearment. He loves her. Or so he believes. She loves him. Or so he believes. I really don't know what she feels or believes. There is trouble in Paradise.

These two have been lovers for several years. They spoke often of marriage during the recent past and even set a target date. It was sometime last summer. The date came and went. He wasn't ready.

There were things to do, not the least of which was getting shed of a wife in some manner he considered decent and as graceful as such shedding ever can be. I'm not sure why time was so essential to that cause — a little more planning, a little better grasp on the future, a little more money socked away for that first wife and his children before taking on the responsibility of the second wife and her children. Time, time, just a little more time.

She decided three or four months ago that time had run out. She told him to get lost.

He has been moping around ever since. Like a punchy fighter, part of his consciousness is frequently in outer space, or inner space. He smiles and hides it pretty well. Not many people know about his sorrow and confusion because not many people knew about his romantic entanglement. I don't think his wife knew. Some men are better at keeping secrets than others. He's very good.

To people who did know, however, he is eager to pour out his misery. It's cathartic. He suffers through the scenario of argument: "She couldn't say she didn't love me; I asked her and she couldn't look me in the eye and say she didn't love me." He details cryptic phone calls, letters, abortive encounters.

He hopes to find some way to undo what he sees as grave damage to their "beautiful life together," which was not a life together at all, just an intimation of one. He wants to get on with it and make it real. So he says.

He grasps at straws, attributing her disenchantment to the brainwashing influence of strangers and business associates. He suggests she really wants to patch it up, but having taken a stand, she is now too proud to back off. He recites a litany of meager evidence to suggest she still cares: He gets phone calls at odd hours but the caller hangs up before speaking; she hasn't asked for her house key back; friends say she looks "unhappy"; her kids say they miss him. A long, explicit and angry letter she wrote him telling him to stop pestering her friends with questions is considered by him proof that she still cares for him very much. She is not indifferent. Therefore, she cares.

All of this is painful for his friends to share. It's like listening to an aging athlete you greatly admire tell you about how he's as good as he ever was, just down on his luck a little bit right now, just a victim of bad breaks, just temporarily out of favor with the coach and the manager. "You wait. They'll realize how great I am. They'll see they can't win without me. They'll put me in the next game, and then I'll show the world! I'll be right back up there on top. Wait and see."

Wait and see. Well, sometimes it happens. You want it to happen, for a friend. Bother morality! You want your friends to have their hearts' desires in everything, including romance. You want them to be happy and content.

Sometimes, however, with eyes clear of romance and dreams, you see things a little more sharply than your friends, and you can't help thinking that what they want is probably not very good for them and hardly worth the cost. Or you see that what your friend wants is actually impossible of attainment. That's the saddest part.

My friend wants the past, as he remembers it, and the future, as he envisioned it. I suspect neither did nor could exist.

That past "beautiful life," even in his own tender recounting of it, appears to have been flawed by recurring misunderstandings, arguments, insecurities, pouts and emotional wrestling matches. Much of this unpleasantness he attributes to the lovers' mutual frustration in not being able to go onward and upward together in marriage. The road to bliss would have undergone a dramatic post-nuptial smoothout, he believes.

Well, maybe. At any rate, the past is done with and nobody can fetch it back. It is impossible for these two people to deny the events and non-events of their lives since December or to play over their mutually inflicted pain. Where do they go from here?

Toward recovery, one hopes. Her course is set. It is independence, however lonely that is for now. That looks healthy to me. He is still threshing about.

Love is not easy, and there is hardly anything rational, adult or even mature about it. It is the same from age 12 to age 102. It is a form of madness which alternately sucks you up toward the sun and drops you down, screaming, into the tar pits. It is an exciting trip, always, and it has never been known to kill anybody. If it wounds, it is only because the victim wants to be wounded or permits it.

It has been estimated that there are something like 4,872 absolutely perfect partners for any person. (I don't know who did the estimating. Somebody told me that.) One hopes that my friend and his lady both hustle out and find a new one. Soon.

— May 2, 1979

Men become husbands: It's a dirty trick

As the World Turns, I get to listen in on the lives of more people than All My Children teetering on the Edge of Night. They write and tell me things. Hum your own organ arpeggio and listen to this:

"My husband is kind, loving, considerate, easy to live with and as liberated as a 45-year-old man can be, but his biggie of the day is to come home to me. I have been underwhelmed by the whole thing. He was a real party boy when I met him, but he turned into a husband when we married — which was a dirty trick."

This correspondent is no disenchanted child bride. She is past the 40-year checkpoint and has been married before.

Can this marriage be saved? These two have a plan. It involves a separation and occasional "mad honeymoon weekends." Barring cardiac arrests, they will either restoke their connubial furnace or it will go out with a phfffft.

When first I read of this domestic crisis, I hooted. Here is a woman sitting in a pot of jam crying for something sweet, thought I. What wife would dislike being the shining hour of her husband's day? Then I thought again. It was the "he turned into a husband" line. I think I know what she means. It IS a dirty trick.

There are husbands who are simply married men. They're keen. Then there are professional husbands. I bet hers is one of the latter. The pros assume a lifestyle and value system along with the title. They're deadly, as are their counterpart professional wives.

The professional husband considers his home his castle and all the boys and girls therein his loyal subjects. This includes his wife. He is not necessarily an Archie Bunker tyrant; he can be a benevolent despot. Either way, he doesn't doubt his divine right to rule.

We'll plant the tree there, paint the shutters blue, watch Monday Night Football and have pot roast on Wednesday. He loves it. He constructed it. Coming home to it and to the compliant wife who keeps it all going according to his plan IS the high point of his day. Wife, however, soon feels like part of the furniture — chosen, purchased and placed by him in the particular corner of his castle he thinks appropriate. She might as well try to hoist an elephant as to change anything.

"Say, Herbie, how about going over to the Hard Rock Cafe tonight for a little boogie. I feel like dancing!"

"Sylvia, darling, I love you but I'm really looking forward to that delicious pot roast of yours and sitting in front of my fire listening to my records on the stereo I built. For us. Why don't you just shuffle around a little bit while you're ironing my shirts. Atta girl. We have a wonderful life, Sylvia. You make me very happy."

Every once in a while one of these pros decides to do something special to reward his chattel. Sometimes it's the gift of a new electric fry pan or a tune-up for her car. Useful things, practical — things that contribute to the smooth operation of the castle and kingdom. Or, it's this:

"Love Bucket, Friday is your birthday. What would you like to do?"

"Oh, Herbie! Go to Samarkand! Wrestle an alligator! Scratch my teeth on a diamond! Surprise me!"

"Well, I thought I would invite your sister and brother-in-law and mother over for a backyard cookout. I'll do the cooking, of course. You enjoy." That means that after she shops for the groceries, fixes the salad and cleans the house, he'll burn some hamburger for the relatives. She'll clean up the mess.

That's the pro. He runs the show. He's a user.

So that I won't be accused of being a female chauvinist, as a male reader once slyly suggested, I'll tell you about the professional wife. She's an almost exact counterpart. She's also a horse pill.

The pro wife devotes her life and all her energy to securing her "catch" (read that "husband") and locking every cell of his body into one of hers. "Together" is a holy word. It goes like this:

"Hi, Shirley. How about meeting me downtown tonight for dinner? Sam and his wife are going to that new Japanese restaurant for the powdered rhinoceros-horn soup. Let's join them. Waddya say?"

"Oh, George. It's soooo expensive. We must remember our budget. Besides, I have your favorite pot roast in our very own oven and I spent the afternoon refinishing your precious golf clubs and monogramming your adorable handkerchiefs. I baked bread for you and made cookies for you and canned peaches for you from our very own peach tree. Come home and enjoy our wonderfulness."

What can he say? Nothing. He goes home. She shows him the His-Her matching needlepoint tennis covers she's made for them and announces they are seeded fifth in the mixed doubles tournament at the club. She's signed him up for Indian Guides, the father-daughter church banquet and the Wednesday night couples potluck and child study club. His parents, and hers, are coming over for Sunday dinner. Is she a wife or is she a wife!

All these people were different before marriage. They had to be. I can't imagine any woman considering marriage to a schmuck who thinks a backyard cookout at home is a peachy birthday present. And no man would knowingly get himself super-glued to a domestic do-do who thinks feathering a nest and sitting in it full time is ecstasy — for both of them.

One assumes that these only slightly exaggerated characters, the pros, play pre-nuptial roles which are then discarded, as nonsense, when they take up the serious business of being married persons. This is the nonsense. And, as my correspondent said, it's a dirty trick.

I suspect that her solution is not going to work, but I think all husbands and wives should at least take a good, honest look at how they behave toward each other today, compared to how they were behaving during the wooing and winning months or years.

If there is much difference, one party or the other is feeling disappointed, trapped and cheated. I guarantee it. That's the trouble. Maybe it's disaster. Maybe it's just a succession of gray days and ho-hum nights until death do you part.

Should we settle for that? Will we be wise enough to change? Will we find the courage to try? Hum another portentous organ arpeggio. That's how these things are done.

— Sept. 9, 1977

Mr. Right becomes Mr. OK, and that seems good enough

There is a young woman I know who has been dating this same young man for over a year now. He's a college graduate with reasonable career prospects. He has a few rough social edges that he is polishing. He's not handsome or dashing. Anyway, what's handsome or dashing? This guy is OK. You understand.

The young woman decided a while back that it is time for her to get married. Her 30th birthday is approaching. She says Mr. OK is an appropriate partner. "Appropriate" is her word.

"What do you think?" she wonders.

I sit staring at my hands. "What difference does it make?" say I.

"Well, you probably have an opinion. I'd like to hear it," she says.

I stare at my hands some more.

I have no opinion on the subject of who ought to marry whom and for what reasons. It's just too confusing.

I presume her no-nonsense approach to matrimony is as good as any, maybe better than most. It wouldn't work for me, but it probably all depends on what you want. I would insist on some fine madness as an essential ingredient. She doesn't.

I used to think that passion and romance were essential to happy marriage. Then I looked around at various marriages — happy, not so happy, miserable — and discovered that the passion part doesn't seem to have much to do with anything.

There are fine marriages involving fine people who display about as much passion for each other as a couple of window washers working opposite sides of the World Trade Center. There are also fine marriages involving fine people who are so huggy-kissy that just being in the same room with them makes your teeth rot.

More interestingly, perhaps, there are plenty of miserable marriages in which passion or romantic love, though present, doesn't make a bug's bit of difference. Obviously, passion and romance can't be essential, despite what we have been so carefully taught in the soaps and movies.

Perhaps romance is just something apart, an ingredient essential to some recipes and superfluous or detrimental to others. Maybe the importance of passion, like the importance of anchovies, depends on the palates of the partners. Some people savor anchovies. Some people can only tolerate them in tiny quantities and prefer not to know they're present at all, thank you.

A marriage, after all, is a partnership contract. Life demands much more than candlelight and huggy-kissy. There is the grass to be cut and the garage to be cleaned. It is a very foolish person who gets suckered by passion and doesn't investigate a potential partner's capacity for doing the necessary work of the marriage business. For the sake of romance and the electricity of sexual attraction, I have seen people marry who otherwise couldn't tolerate each other for a long weekend at the lake. Sometimes it works; sometimes it doesn't. That's the mystery and puzzlement.

Certainly some consideration of the appropriateness of the union, outside the romantic part, is sensible. My pal who is pondering marriage to Mr. OK is remarkably sensible. She has never once mentioned love. She has not talked about how Mr. OK glows in the dark or about how she likes the taste and smell of him. She hasn't said he makes her laugh and feel she's very special, or that she just likes to look at him because he seems so beautiful . . . washing the car . . . reading the newspaper.

What do I think about this marriage? Nothing. I wish it well, but it is as alien to me as a marriage of Martians. More and more, however, I feel that I am probably a displaced Venusian, so what do I know about marriage on this, or any planet? Only a couple of things for certain: Marriage is the most difficult task undertaken by human beings. A successful, happy marriage is a rare and awesome construction, for which there is still no blueprint or formula. How strange that so many people attempt the construction at all, and with such innocent optimism.

— May 13, 1981

Lunch bunch's dilemma: 'Not tonight, Sweetheart'

A male reader who identifies himself as "a middle-aged professional" wrote recently to ask if a man is justified telling his wife, "Not tonight, Sweetheart, I have a headache" — or is that insensitive and selfish? Would it precipitate suspicion, generate feminine anger or, perhaps, bring on an attack of the Poor Me pouts?

He says a bunch of the boys discussed this question over their martini and London broil recently and couldn't agree. They did agree that each of them had faced the dilemma more than once.

"We all love our wives," he wrote, "and find them attractive and sexy. It's just that we don't always feel like sex when they do, and with all this women's lib, they can come on rather strong at times."

I got the giggles reading his letter. I wasn't laughing at him, or the problem, but at images in my mind of Walter Matthau feigning migraine under the quivering, flapping sheets in order to fend off the determined sexual overtures of, let's say, Carol Burnett.

"Oooohhh," he moans, clutching his head. "Not now, not now . . . tomorrow . . . maybe next week . . . ohhh . . . "

"Poor baby," says she, moving closer. "Does Itsey Bitsey Boopsie Oopsie have a big, bad boo-boo? Let Moochey Woochey kiss it and make it all well . . ."

I also remembered an old magazine cartoon in which a graying, balding and definitely paunchy gentleman with a walrus mustache lay flat on his back in bed, staring morosely at the ceiling. His equally graying and paunchy wife lay in an identical posture next to him. Both wore baggy night shirts but she had black, spike-heeled boots on her feet. "Is this as kinky as it gets, Edgar?" said she.

What's farce in print or film can be melodrama in real life. I do sympathize with the troubled lunch bunch, as well as their wives.

We have all studied the sensible sex therapists' advice. Be honest. Don't fake. Be loving. Don't snub. Say "yes" when you feel like it and "no" when you don't. Ask for what you want; decline when you can't participate comfortably. Be affectionate and communicative and reassuring at all times, however. And when you must decline an invitation, or things just aren't working out, try snuggling and

too. Why then is it so difficult for
osephine," to their amorous wives?
e same reasons generations of wives
ot tonight, Joe," to their husbands and
ge of splitting headaches or nagging back-

'd to admit we are not each Don Juan or Nora
the cool pool. Almost every aspect of our culture
tly or openly that healthy American men and women
ing more than energetic sex, at almost any hour of the day
and in preference to almost any other activity.

en are supposed to forget urgent appointments at the Chase
anhattan Bank whenever they see a woman flounce past wearing
her Hanes pantyhose. Gentlemen prefer them, you see.

Women are supposed to recover miraculously from hours of floor scrubbing, whisk off their aprons and become panting felines in anticipation of an Ambiance night.

We are supposed to fall into each others' arms with no more provocation than a whiff of Wind Song or a glimpse of a Close-Up smile. Brighter teeth and fresher breath will get Sylvia back, Oscar!

It's easy enough to tell ourselves all of this is nonsense, but we are so steeped in the myth that in bed, with the lights low and the dreamy music wafting from the stereo, it is a jolt to find that sex is not always more fun than anything.

The mind, both male and female, begins thinking something is wrong with him, or me, or her or us. To say "no" is to reject the partner's sexual appeal or expertise. To say "no" is to deny one's own sexual appetite and, therefore, sexual desirability. In short, a person who says "no" feels he or she just isn't normal or healthy.

Even when our minds tell us that all of this is as dopey as the perfume ads, we are never sure our partners know it's dopey. So we invent headaches to protect their egos and our own. I guess we are dopey enough to think the lie works. It never does.

Truth works. So, yes, it's just fine for middle-aged or any other men to say, "Not tonight, Sweetheart," so long as they shrug, smile and hug a lot. If you ask their wives. I bet they'd agree. It is such a relief not to be the Geritol couple.

— *March 23, 1979*

Tears of mourning as much as joy

A Berkley High School teacher wonders why people cry weddings. Actually, she is not the primary wonderer. One of h students did the initial wondering and asked the teacher about i and the teacher tossed it to me. Do I have any ideas on this subject? But, of course.

People cry at weddings because they are in a highly agitated, near hysterical state. This is especially true of parents of brides and grooms, grandparents of brides and grooms and, often, sisters and best friends of brides and grooms and assorted guests. Brothers of the principals are generally less severely affected. Aunts, uncles and cousins rarely show any symptoms at all.

It is unclear whether the tears and blubbering are joyful. I suspect some are not; at least not in the whoopee sense of joyful.

We may as well examine the emotional state of the bride and groom first. There are occasional exceptions, but these two principal actors in the wedding drama are usually either highly manic or near catatonic by the time wedding guests begin to assemble. There is hardly ever any emotional middle ground. All circuits are over-loaded.

I heard about one groom who was so zombie-like during the hours immediately preceding his nuptials that he absent-mindedly shut his cat up in his refrigerator. Fortunately, the animal was discovered and released by a second party within a relatively short period of time, shivering and indignant, but otherwise unharmed.

A certain bride who shall remain nameless was so afflicted with pre-wedding twitches she ran three pairs of hose (every pair she owned that wasn't packed for her honeymoon trip) attempting to don her wedding finery. She collapsed in tears and told her mother to call off the ceremony. How could she possibly go through with this thing when she couldn't even get dressed? She meant it. Pathetic.

It is not meaningless form which prescribes a Best Man and Maid of Honor. These two are supposed to be responsible persons who will think for the principals, button their buttons, zip their zippers, point them in the right direction at the right time and discourage each from running off alone to join the circus, which always looks increasingly more attractive as the appointed wedding hour approaches.

Brides and grooms rarely weep at their own weddings, however. They are too numb. They have a sense of being actors or marionettes. They want to produce a good show to remember on future wedding anniversaries (they rarely remember much of it) and to please their families and guests. Mostly they want to get this very significant, very serious, very disorienting business over with so they can breathe again.

It is in the church or synagogue or the gussied-up living room of Aunt Sophie's house with the officiating person standing tall and at the ready and the bride (with plastic smile) approaching the groom (with plastic smile) to the strains of Wagner or Mancini that the tears begin.

I have made a study of this. They first well up in the eyes of the mothers of the bride and groom. This happens more or less simultaneously. Next, it's the father of the bride who begins to sniffle. After this and in rapid succession come the tears of the father of the groom, any immediately pre- or post-pubescent sisters of the principals, sorority sisters of the bride, older brothers of the bride or the groom, and, sometimes, grandfathers. Little brothers and grandmothers rarely cry. They smile a lot.

I think the little brothers and grandmothers are genuinely happy for everybody and everything. I think they get a boot out of the flowers and the pretty clothes and the pageant. I don't think they feel any sense of loss. Almost everyone else does — except the bride and groom.

Mothers and fathers lose their children. The children are obviously grown up, no longer owing emotional allegiance primarily to Mom and Dad. There is now this spouse who has first call. In losing the child, the parent loses some of his or her own body, time and usefulness. It is a joyful parting, one hopes, but the tears are tears of mourning as much as joy.

Unmarried brothers and sisters of the principals lose one of their own kind, to a different status; married brothers and sisters welcome a new member of the club. There are ironic tears for the high hope of perfect union, which almost all present know is impossible to achieve.

There are tears shed in remembrance of past personal joys and sorrows. Tears for dreams each innocent hopes will come true mingle with tears of disillusionment each semi-jaded witness sheds for bliss unrealized.

All of this, I contend, is why people cry at weddings and why they say, "I don't know why I'm crying; it's all so beautiful and I'm happy for them." Tears at weddings are shed for the beauty of every bright promise and for the simultaneous intuition which tells us few are ever fully realized.

The best and brightest tears are shed smilingly and in awe of the courage and love which attempts all of this anyway.

— *April 4, 1979*

Falling short of the ideal is no longer a high crime

Sexual fidelity to one's marriage partner is still the ideal in American society. It may still be the norm. Admitting one has fallen short of the ideal or failed to comply with the norm, however, no longer amounts to screeching scandal. I learned this recently reading newspapers and watching TV.

Twice in the past month, American men assigned to overseas diplomatic service have said Russian agents maneuvered them into sexual encounters with women other than their wives. The Russians then attempted to use evidence of these dalliances to get the Americans to pass along secret information.

Neither entrapment worked. Both times the Americans promptly reported the attempted blackmail to their superiors. No strong effort was made by the men or by American authorities to conceal the sexual nature of the shenanigans. After a day or two of seemingly mild embarrassment all around, the men were reassigned.

It may take a while for divorce papers to be filed. We may never know the weeping and wailing, accusations and counter-accusations that go on in the privacy of these diplomatic attaches' homes. For now, however, it appears their lives and the lives of their families are proceeding without a hiccup.

Not so long ago, major novels and high-budget motion pictures were woven around the perceived catastrophe of marital infidelity, usually called adultery. The attempts of pitiable or despicable characters to salvage themselves after a romp in the sheets with an attractive stranger were grim. Murder and financial ruin always loomed large, and the tragic dissolution of marriage was absolutely guaranteed.

I suspect these books and movies were an accurate reflection of a widely held viewpoint, which we may now have outgrown or modified.

The open, candid revelation by our diplomats of this bungled Russian blackmail is one evidence. The public's failure to respond with much more than raised eyebrows followed by, "What else is new?" is another.

If I knew a blackmailer, I would ask about this. Is it still possible to extort money from a weary traveler who shares his bed with a stranger? Do men still quake at the prospect of their wives being shown the incriminating photographs? Do wives quake for ditto reasons? Do spouses suffer mental breakdowns or succumb to murderous urges when the awful truth is revealed?

I suppose some do and some don't. I suspect, however, there is less likelihood of the extremes of human outrage now than ever before.

For one thing, we have had 30 years to digest the findings of the Kinsey Report and all the sexual research that followed. We have learned by osmosis, if not through direct study, that monogamous fidelity is much more common among Canada geese than among American males and females. Never mind what the fairy tales and romantic movies purport.

We have learned that sex is sometimes perceived by many otherwise admirable males as recreational activity and not always as a sacred intimacy to be shared exclusively by husband and wife. We have learned that women, too, have strong sexual appetites and that many otherwise admirable women are as capable as men of enjoying casual sexual encounters.

We have witnessed the still burgeoning sexual liberation of women, in part because of the availability of reliable contraceptives and in part because women are less financially dependent upon men now.

This is not to say that many or all of us have accepted this new morality as a personal lifestyle. As noted, fidelity in marriage is still the ideal and, perhaps, the norm.

But I believe society in general has come to view occasional infidelity, especially male infidelity, with less horror and alarm than our grandmothers did or could. I suspect we are much more likely to forgive, almost without prejudice, when we are convinced the fooling around was a one-time-only thing.

I'm not sure if this sort of charity is a mark of social progress or decay. My vote goes with progress, but the jury is still out.

— Feb. 25, 1981

Where's a house-husband when you really need him?

Enlightenment visits itself upon the human mind in flickers and flashes, sometimes late at night.

What follows is a more or less accurate account of the conversation of three professional women, all working in their shared office late into one recent evening.

Mary: Sweet heaven (yawn) . . . what are we doing here? We are supposed to be stars. Why are we still at our desks at 8:30 p.m.?

Jane: (Wearily) Because that's what makes us stars.

(Long silence during which work continues.)

Carol: (Stuffing papers in a briefcase) Well, that's it for me. Now, all I want is a good back rub and somebody to feed me dinner.

Jane: And maybe a glass of champagne.

Mary: (Sighs) A Filipino house boy. I want one of those, white coat and all. He would keep the house in perfect order, cook and serve meals, do my laundry . . .

Carol: . . . take the dry cleaning out and pick it up, deal with the plumber, never be whiney or demanding . . .

Jane: You know what we're talking about, don't you? We want wives. The old-fashioned kind.

(Laughter)

Carol: Yes, but real wives aren't like that.

Mary and Jane (unison): Some of them are! (Laughter)

Mary: (sighs) Remember all the times we wondered why those men with all the charm and brains — the ones with the good, tough jobs we drooled over — we wondered why in hell they always wound up marrying adoring, unaspiring yo-yos? That's it. Those men are just like us. They want just what we want. Somebody to rub their feet. Somebody to hand them a martini, smile, cook their favorite foods, look pretty and have it all ready when they come home at 10 p.m., beat.

Jane: Well, I can certainly understand that. And they're right. (Looks at clock which now reads 9:20 p.m.) Tell me what man in his right mind would want to marry one of us?

(Laughter)

That's the end of the playlet and the beginning of the enlightenment.

Where are the house-husbands for career women? If there are women content to dedicate their lives to the domestic comfort and pleasure of their tycoon husbands, where are the counterpart men for tycoon wives? Nowhere, or hiding out.

I know of one marriage which is supposed to be working that way, but it isn't. The husband has a demanding part-time job and the wife still performs a lot of traditional wifely chores. I know another in which the man says he would be perfectly content to fulfill the traditional housewife role to his vice-president mate. But he doesn't. And he could. So I don't believe him.

All this presents a dilemma to the dedicated feminist.

As any committed career woman who can fantasize must realize, it would be wonderful to come home to that clean, orderly house, the martini, the back rub, the smiling, uncritical, unchallenging, non-competitive comforter. If the comforter were also handsome and loving, yahoo! Who cares if he isn't smart? Who needs him famous? Smart and famous would ruin everything. He'd start getting uppity.

When you start fantasizing about a house-husband, it is easy to see why a lot of men got very angry at a lot of feminists a decade or so ago. Imagine having your very own, handsome, adoring house-husband who actually believes God and nature designed him to this purpose. There he is carefully washing out your pantyhose while you read Playgirl magazine (for the articles) and sip your strawberry daiquiri. Then some Duke Wayne macho-type from next door comes in and starts preaching to your husband:

"Fred, think, man! You should go back to college and get that degree you gave up when you married her. It doesn't matter that she's a good provider and appreciates what you do around the house and is good to you. What's that? Where's your pride, man? You are dependent. Get yourself an identity of your own. You are being exploited and repressed in this marriage. Put down that frying pan. If your wife is hungry, let her learn to cook. You did. She can learn how to do the laundry and run the vacuum, too. Why should you wait on her when she comes home? You have a right to realize your potential!"

There goes paradise. Aarrrrrgh.

The pure truth is that there are still women around who are willing to become submissive housewives, so the powerful and demanding male can usually find just what he wants. Able-bodied, capable and dedicated house-husbands, however, are about as commonplace as unicorns. How depressing for emerging female tycoons. Women even have an uphill fight becoming Female Chauvinist Pigs.

— June 30, 1980

Portraits of four marriages don't make pretty pictures

Sometimes I don't think anybody knows anything for sure, especially about love, marriage and the dissolution of same.

I asked a marriage counselor once to tell me the major cause of divorce. He thought aloud for a minute, discarding such things as money squabbles, extra-marital affairs and arguments over jobs and kids. "Boredom," he said finally.

Boredom?

I asked four divorced people I know what finally ripped it for them. None mentioned boredom. The answers were surprising, and sad:

"I always bought my own cars and my own clothes," said a woman who was married about 15 years. She explained her husband had always earned a considerable income. He handled all the family finances. He paid for everything, except his wife. She had a small, independent income and, although she never asked to keep her money separate from his, that's how he preferred it.

"Money was very important to him, and when I realized he wasn't spending a dime on me, I realized he didn't care anything about me, even though he said he did and maybe even thought he did. He used to just hand me the Saks bills and say, 'How do you want to handle this?' When I needed a new car he'd say. 'Well, how much do you think you can afford to spend?'

"I was like a boarder in his house. He bought golf clubs and convertibles and sailboats and anything he wanted, but he never even bought my clothes. I felt exploited, and I finally decided the hugs weren't worth the compromises I had to make and the humiliation I felt in that boarding house. I left."

Another woman's lament: "He always had an eye for beautiful women. I mean, he appreciated them. At parties and everywhere, he was always ogling the fashion-model types and telling them how lovely they were. I wasn't jealous. I knew he was just looking. But I'm not exactly chopped liver either.

"When we were married, I tried very hard to be pretty, and I was. I still am. Anyway, we were married 12 years, and in all that time he never once told me I was pretty, let alone anything more. Other men told me I was attractive. I thought I deserved to be special, to my husband more than anybody. I hated him for withholding the praise and appreciation that he seemed to lavish on total strangers. It was giving me a terrible inferiority complex. I had to get out."

A man's complaint: "She never came to bed naked. She was always in some dumb nightgown, not even a sexy one. There was a pink flannel thing. I especially remember. Totally sexless, really ugly. Every night she'd go into the bathroom to undress and put on some nightgown. Can you imagine that? The bathroom! I never saw her standing there in front of me naked.

"Anyway, then she'd come to bed in the dark, and we'd have to wrestle the damn nightgown off and later, after we had sex, she'd get out of bed and put the nightgown back on again. I wanted to hold her body next to mine — go to sleep that way. The nightgown was always there. I finally blew up about it. She said she got cold at night. Hell, we had an electric blanket. It was just her way of shutting me out, keeping me away.

"So, finally I decided she ought to have what she wanted."

Finally, there's this from another man: "She never wanted to rub suntan lotion on my body. I know that sounds like a strange reason to end a marriage, but when I think about it I always come back to that. It says something, you know? It says she didn't like me, the physical part. She didn't take any pleasure in touching my body. It finally was just too important to get around."

The above four responses represent my typical exhaustive research. You will note, however, that no one mentioned boredom. Which makes me wonder how much marriage counselors really know and can know. Maybe it depends on how honest their clients are.

— *May 22, 1981*

Courtship uses lots of energy but provides little return

He is married and the father of three school-age kids. He loves them. He likes his wife and respects her talents as a homemaker and mother. He is proud of her going back to school part-time to work toward the college degree she abandoned for marriage 15 years ago. He's not sure whether he loves this wife, however.

He didn't think about love much, until recently. About a year ago he met a young, pretty, single woman at his work place. He fancied himself in love. These two carried on a leisurely affair for about six or eight months.

"I've been thinking about a divorce," he told me once, a while back. "Is there a good or bad time for it? I mean, is it easier on the kids now, or should I wait until they're older? What do you think?"

"I think you are playing romantic games," I told him. "If you are ready for a divorce you'll know it. It's like an ulcer. It hurts and it doesn't go away. Pretty soon you can't fret anymore about the timing or the effect on the kids or the boss or even the bank balance. It won't even matter if the Tootsie in your life runs off with a saxophone player. The worst thing you can imagine happening will still be better than staying married. That's how it feels."

"Yeah?" he said.

"I think so," I said.

I hadn't seen this person again for about four months, until last week. I asked him about his divorce. He grinned. No divorce. No more Tootsie. He had lost interest. The storm was over, or he had hit the eye of it. At any rate, life was going on as usual, pretty good, if predictable.

I wondered about the woman, in whom he had lost interest. I didn't know her, so I was free to imagine her variously. She was good, kind, trusting and faithful. She was rotten, demanding, manipulative and scornful. She was sad or relieved. She could be anything. I was glad for her, and for him, that the interlude was over.

Nothing happens to anyone in the electric, explosive initial stage of a loving relationship. Hearts pound, eyes sparkle, skins shiver and the sex is splendid (or pretty good). Two people who are so very special to each other do lots of things together which seem exciting and wonderful, but they don't actually do much of any consequence. Courtship and early love are the most fallow times in people's lives.

We are a lot like chickens in this regard. So it seems to me. When we are courting and in the throes of romance, we hardly have time, consciousness or energy to do anything except preen and posture for the beloved. Display behavior is very important. Sensual pleasure is dynamite. We spend a lot of time lollygagging over and around each other.

What we don't do is build a house together. That comes later, after the heat is off. We don't plant a garden or plan a future. We don't start a business or close one up. We don't go about the necessary, everyday chores and concerns of living because that's pretty boring and ordinary stuff compared to the phosphorescent shimmer of new love.

Unfortunately, after a while, it is very hard to sustain the magic moments, partly because a great deal of the magic depends on mystery and discovery. After most of the mysteries of another person are solved and most of the discoveries are made, a great deal of the magic just naturally evaporates. Now it's time to build the house or plant the garden or, probably, have the babies. It is impossible for the electricity to continue sparking. For most people the end of the white hot courtship comes as a relief. It takes a lot of energy and produces little return.

That's why I was happy for my friend and his lady. They could now go their separate ways and get on with the business of living. He could go back to his wife and kids, whom he does love whether he understands it or not. She could go on, perhaps to another romance which has a chance of settling into a friendly, loving, co-operative partnership.

I knew a woman once who thought herself in love with a married man, who thought himself in love with her. These two carried on a flashy affair for more than 10 years. It was always thrilling; it never changed. When it finally ended, it was as if they had never known each other. They made that little difference in each other's lives or the world at large. Interesting, I thought. And still do.

— Feb. 21, 1979

A marriage license
and three postcards

It is too easy to get married and too difficult to get divorced. I
have figured this out over several years of listening to the whimper-
ings of otherwise pleasant people who have stumbled on one or the
other of these thresholds.

As things are presently organized, any two venereally healthy
lummoxes over the age of 18 and of opposite sex are legally entitled
to become husband and wife, no questions asked. All they have to do
is scrape up $5 between them and find their way to the county clerk's
office. That's what I call easy.

Later, however, when Lummox One discovers that Lummox Two
is unnaturally attracted to chickens and breeds cockroaches as a
hobby, too bad! The state, the church, Aunt Myrtle and everybody in
the bowling league agrees the Lummoxes owe it to themselves and
society to hang together.

In order to get unmarried, the Lummoxes must deal with the
weird sisters — lawyers, judges and critical relatives. This is tough.
There are lists of pots and pans to be made, disclosures of money do-
ings, arguments, justifications, haggles, judgments and decrees. All
this takes a long time and costs much more than $5. The toll in emo-
tional currency is unmeasurable.

None of this makes sense. If marriage is a sacred and serious
business as we are given to believe, how come there aren't prerequi-
sites to it? Where are the lectures, courses, examinations and final
certification procedure so that nobody can get married unless he or
she has the proper credentials? If an honest disclosure and dispersal
of assets is required to get out of a marriage, why is there no such requirement for getting into one?

Well, there isn't and probably never will be. To do all this would
shatter the Cinderella syndrome which we have come to know and
love. We are all going to fall in love with a beautiful stranger at first
sight, ride off into the sunset and live happily ever after.

Me too. So, I give up on that end of the process.

As for the other end — the exit door — I have a dandy idea. It is
fair and it is honest and it might actually encourage domestic

tranquility, even among Lummoxes.

What we do is make getting a divorce at least as easy as getting married. We take it out of the legal arena. Since we leave it to the individuals concerned to decide if and when they will marry and for what reasons, this scheme leaves it to the individuals concerned to decide if and when and for what reasons they will divorce.

What we do is issue everybody, men and women, three postcards at the same time we issue them a marriage license. These postcards are to be carried on the person at all times, sort of like a driver's license, in triplicate. It's the law! The cards have computer-coded numbers printed on them, and somewhere in the heartland of the U.S. — say, in Atchison, Kan. — is a giant memory bank in which is stored your individual marriage license number, plus the numbers on these three postcards.

The postcards are pre-printed. No. 1 says, "I'm not happy with this marriage." No. 2 says, "Divorce is looking better and better." No. 3 says, "That's it. I divorce you."

As the Lummoxes blunder along the rocky marriage road and find difficulties which they can't talk or shout out together, each has the ever-present knowledge that all it takes to get out of this mess forever is to mail the cards, in succession to the spouse.

As the cards go through the U.S. mail system, the numbers are electronically read and flashed to the computer in Kansas. Click, whirrr, buzzz. It is duly noted that warning one has been issued to Leonard Lummox by his present wife, Louise.

Of course, one postcard is not enough to accomplish the divorce deed. All three must be mailed — yellow alert, then red, then blackout. I suspect husbands might be a little more considerate of wives, and vice versa, if each knew that this simple unilateral action is all it takes to dissolve a marriage.

It would be easy to know just which verbal blast was an idle threat and which was serious. Did you get a card in the mail? It would be dangerous to be a horse's derriere on a regular basis figuring the spouse will put up with it. Maybe not. Did you get a card in the mail?

There are added benefits to society at large, too. Since the law will require that we all carry our postcards with us at all times, it will be much more difficult for married persons to fool around, telling those sweet-sounding lies.

"My marriage is falling apart, Gumdrop," he'll say. "My wife doesn't understand me and we live as Monk and Nun. It is you I love;

trust me."

"Let's mail a postcard together," she'll say coyly. Gotcha!

There are a few details to be worked out. Once the divorce is accomplished, post-paid, I haven't figured out how to divvy up the household goods. I thought maybe they could be confiscated by the state and sold at auction or something. The previously married Lummoxes could be given equal shares of the proceeds, minus expenses. Something like that. I don't want any bickering over who gets which car.

I also don't know what to do about persons who skip town and leave no forwarding addresses. Maybe the IRS could find them. Minor details. I am convinced the postcard idea has at least as much merit as the present legal system. Cheaper, too.

— Oct. 20, 1978

Married swains play hide-and-seek

The doorbell rings and in pops Carol, fuming. "The liar. I knew he was married the minute he suggested a restaurant halfway to Port Huron," she says. She had a dinner date with a new man. "He admitted it and then had the nerve to say it doesn't matter because he has Mondays free. Mondays!"

Carol told her would-be lover that she has Monday through Sunday free and is looking for a similarly situated man. Thanks for dinner.

Mom was right. Married men can be a trap and a snare.

I had conversations recently with four or five unmarried women who have experienced the displeasure. Some have participated in long-term affairs; some have sampled briefly; some are in the throes.

Morals and ethics are the purview of the theologians and philosophers. I'm a curbstone pragmatist. Any man and woman who have a warm, mutually satisfying relationship are OK with me. I'm not going to worry about whether they are married to each other or to one or two other people.

The hook in there is the "mutually satisfying" part. There is a commonality of gripes expressed by single women about such arrangements, however, and gripers are not satisfied souls.

Chief among these complaints is loneliness. "My apartment has never been so clean," says one wistful female. "I have all day Saturday and Sunday to scrub it." She's in the throes.

Weekends are for families, and legitimate couples. Mr. Marvelous is painting his garage, fixing his back porch and escorting his wife and kids to parties and parks. He doesn't mind; he enjoys it. It salves his conscience.

Miss Wonderful is supposed to be content at home alone, visiting Aunt Minnie. At their next encounter, Marvie will say, "I thought about you all weekend, darling." She should say, "I thought about you, too, and it was like watching paint dry." She probably won't.

No man, married or single, is worth the emotional investment to any woman, married or single, if he has more important things to do every Saturday and Sunday than be with her. An occasional golf game is OK. More than that and I would hie myself off to play polo with Prince Philip, should he be in the neighborhood.

I also dislike the game of hide-and-seek which married swains play. Carol was a victim.

He says, "Sweetheart, let's spend Thursday together. We can have dinner and do whatever you like." He doesn't mean that. He means, we can have dinner and do whatever you like as long as it's in a remote part of Delaware where there is no chance of anybody I know seeing me.

I once had such a dinner arrangement. We went to a restaurant that closed a week later because it hadn't had 10 customers during the previous three years. We were solitary diners. Whispers echoed. He called it "romantic" and a "gourmet place." I called it spooky. So much for him.

What's worse, my research indicates that no matter what the night's delights, Mr. M. pulls himself together by 2 a.m. when his cover, the bars and bistros, close. He heads home. He doesn't want a fight. This is universally unsatisfactory to the women I know.

To make up for such unpleasantness, philanderers of means sometimes play World Class hide-and-seek. They pop for airplane tickets and hotel suites in New York or even London. It's business.

Less-flush Lotharios go "fishing with the boys" and really drive "the girls" to Chicago. This may be romantic and relaxing a couple of times a year, but what does she do when she wants to go to a Fisher Theatre opening? She doesn't, with him. Phooey.

I can't say that all romantic relationships between married men and unmarried women are unsatisfactory. All of them are less than complete or ideal, however.

Women put up with them when they can't find anything better, i.e. single. Or, women enjoy them because all they want is a sometime thing. Every once in a while, there may be a married man who doesn't suffer from the usual inhibitions. They don't have signs on them unfortunately.

I have a rule of thumb in human encounters which may be useful: When you get less pleasure than pain from an alliance, it's time to get out. It goes for both sexes and all relationships.

Women especially need to think about these things.

A friend of mine named Bill recently got a call from a married man who said, "I just put Henrietta on the plane for Florida. You know a lot of single girls. How 'bout you fixing me up with somebody and we'll go out and swing a little?"

To his everlasting credit, Bill said, "If I run into a single woman who wants to go to bed with a married man, once, and never have him call her again — I'll let you know." Let's hear it for Bill out there, folks. I'd introduce him to Carol except that Bill's already got a girl. Naturally.

— March 14, 1977

Phooey on the little boxes other people put around us

I used to live in a lot of little boxes. Now I live in one, and it's commodious. I designed, built and decorated it. Sometimes I kick out a side or two and rearrange the dimensions and decor. I do this when I get tired of the same environment or it becomes uncomfortable or I get excited about some change I have observed or envisioned and decide to experiment. The box may not suit you at all. It suits me, and I live in it. It's my life. It's labeled "Nickie."

As noted, I used to live in a lot of little boxes. They had labels, too. One was "The Kids." One was "Husband." There were "Relatives," "The Boss," "Neighbors," "Friends & Associates," "Church & Society." There may have been some others, but these were the important ones, as I recall.

I remember spending a lot of energy climbing from one box to another and catching my breath after each scramble. I was often disoriented. I frequently felt cramped and uncomfortable.

"What's she talking about, Irma?"

"I have no idea, Frank. McWhirter is sometimes hard to follow."

I'll try to explain. You see, these little boxes were all constructed by other people. They were made out of ideas and concepts. The one labeled "Relatives" was constructed by my parents and other relatives, and when I was inside I had to contort and ooze myself into a configuration which fit the interior. I had to become a person who conformed to these relatives' ideas of what constituted the best possible me. When I was in the box labeled "Husband" "Kids" or any of the others, I had to become a person who fit that box, even though there wasn't room for my elbows or knees.

You see how uncomfortable living in boxes can be, especially since I had to keep skipping from one to another, and a stance which worked well in one box might be totally unlivable in the next.

I mean, what do you do when the kids expect the Perfect You to play backyard baseball and at the same time husband wants you to entertain customers and boss expects you to be at work and the family thinks it's time you invited them up to have a backyard cookout with the neighbors before going to the church ice cream social where you are expected to play hostess — after you have put in your time as a volunteer at the library, naturally, and collected money for the Pigmy Relief Fund? Never mind your friends who say you never see them any more and have gotten "uppity."

Phooey on boxes. A person can get terminal shinsplints climbing in and out and trying to conform. I quit some time ago.

It wasn't because I minded the energy required or was unsympathetic with the box makers. I quit living in the boxes because disappointment and discontent were inevitable all around.

It is possible for any human being to live in a single box, designed by its occupant or even by somebody else, but it is not possible to live in more than one box at a time. I decided that after years of research and observation of others engaged in this struggle.

It is difficult to become a Contented You in a box designed by someone else, but there is evidence that this is sometimes possible. It has been accomplished by some nuns, priests and assorted other clerics and religious persons. Beyond this, I know of a few women who play Galatea to their Pygmalion husbands and appear to thrive. (I know of no male-female reversal of these roles which has succeeded but am willing to concede the possibility.)

For most of us, however, what happens is that we disappoint the many who construct boxes for us to occupy because, in fulfilling the demands of one, we leave empty places in the constructions of others. And when we try to fulfill the expectations of only one person or group outside ourselves we find we have to stretch uncomfortably to reach some of the corners and cramp ourselves up unnaturally to fit into some of the tight spots.

It's much better if each of us designs his or her own box, or life. It can be spacious or cozy. It can have many compartments or few; they can be locked and private or open to the public. The important consideration is that the life is comfortable and pleasing to the occupant. It is custom-made; one of a kind. It doesn't pinch and bind or require the person to go about stooped and bent, anxious, hurting, worrisome and feeling inadequate to the demands and expectations of others. If we do not learn to construct our own lives and reject the pre-fab jobs so eagerly foisted off on us by others — even for good and noble reasons — we'll never feel comfortable in the house that has the many mansions. We won't recognize which one is ours.

— *Aug. 13, 1978*

Riches and whisky —
and a search for love

I have a friend who is in a hospital being kept alive by doctors, nurses and machines that go click, click in measured, impersonal electronic cadences. When the liver is shot along with the kidneys and pancreas and various other necessary parts, the agony of DTs is a minor complication.

The doctors are trying to salvage some function from these vital organs and keep his heart and lungs working at the same time. If they succeed, they may buy time to deal with the crippling malnutrition, irreversible damage to the nervous and digestive systems and God knows what else.

My friend can't have visitors. He is only semi-conscious and the slightest exertion further threatens his life.

A lot of people who know him would say he's getting what he asked for, and deserves.

They remember a foul-mouthed, bad-smelling drunk, dressed like a bum, bouncing off walls in private clubs and the best watering spots in town. He embarrassed them.

Long ago, they crossed him off the invitation lists. He had the audacity to keep showing up at the Detroit Athletic Club, the Country Club and the Chop House whenever he chose. He couldn't hit bottom. He outraged a lot of people.

Some put up with his appearance and his abuse in the name of good manners. They made small talk with him and pretended in his presence that he was fine, just fine. Later they would gossip among themselves about his every indiscretion.

He knew it. He said he didn't care, but he hated it and never understood this particular savagery.

There was no way to make him understand that he reminded people of their own inadequacies and, especially, of their greed.

People could not and cannot forgive him for having and wasting so much of what they covet. He had it all.

There was inherited wealth measured in the millions of dollars, plus ancestors of power, style and accomplishment. There were good schools, fine houses, servants and all the "advantages," many of which he disdained.

He was handsome — tall and strong with dark hair and eyes as blue as the Arizona sky.

His appetites were large, his curiosity insatiable. He climbed the Himalayas and trekked through Afghanistan. He flew to England for Ascot and watched the races from the royal enclosure. He owned and learned to fly a hot air balloon and shot the white water on the middle fork of the Salmon River.

He skied the most unforgiving mountains in the world. His toys were motorcycles and ocean race boats and Alfa Romeo sport cars. There were a lot of women.

He thought little of spending $1,000 a day to charter a yacht to explore the Mediterranean for a month, or thousands more to bound about Paris on a whim or Morocco on a dare.

His favorite meal began with beluga and ended with crepes suzette and heaven help the waiter who provided too few lemons for the fish eggs or too much Grand Marnier for the pancakes.

He disdained the morals of God and the manners of man. He was an irritant to people of conventional wealth with conventional values and conventional appetites. He was insufferable.

"Such a waste," they say and cluck their tongues and recount his excuses. "So weak. So self-indulgent. So self-destructive."

In all of his extravagance, in his squandering of life, my friend was groping for the one thing he couldn't buy. He never knew how to give or receive love. He substituted everything for that.

Long before he got his nose stuck in a bottle, he sensed the hollow in his soul. It confused and troubled him.

He tried to love a wife and ultimately lost her. He wanted to be a good father to his two children, but he didn't know how.

He could never please his own father, or his mother, or a succession of girlfriends who wanted little except to adore him and be kept in comfort.

There was an emptiness where the love should have been. It was eradicated early, as completely as a hand is lost to a punch press.

Whisky was his solace.

It helped him think he was loved when he wasn't; it helped him think he loved someone when he didn't.

It helped him think he had friends and that they were genuine even when they cheated him and tricked him. It put him to sleep and it woke him up.

When he couldn't sort any of his life out any more, whisky helped him not to care. And it took a terrible toll.

Because he couldn't love himself, he ignored the swollen feet and yellow cast to his eyes and the warnings of doctors. He believed he was invincible, that he could live on will alone.

He would have continued his agonizing search and I admire his spirit beyond telling.

But that is over. Whisky has quenched the fire. What is left of my friend is not what there was before. There will still be mountains, but someone else will climb them.

With luck, there may be small pleasures left to him; people will be hired to care. He used to like azaleas, watching a cat named Frog, reading, talking with children and fixing things with his hands. I hope these things are left to him.

— Feb. 18, 1977

A few days after this column was written, my friend died. He had few friends left. He was 36 years old.

Only your body knows why you are magnetized to water

Maybe you've noticed. Nobody turns his or her back to a body of water. We can ignore skyscrapers and wheat fields, finding them boring by and by. Given enough time even the mountains and the forests become almost invisible through familiarity. We are mesmerized by water throughout our lifetimes, however.

Ocean, lake, river, winding stream, the creek in the backyard, the swimming pool at the park, even large fountains and small reflecting pools — if it's water and it's there, we face it. We watch it. We can't be distracted from it for long, and the position of privilege is almost always the one closest to the edge of the wet.

Wherever we find ourselves, however, our eyes will scan the surface of any nearby water and flicker again and again to its lapping edges. Nothing, from conversation to games to the book we brought along and thought we would read, commands our total attention as long as water is nearby. The presence of water overrides that of anybody or anything else.

The most desirable homes have an ocean, river or lake view. The most desirable hotels have an ocean, river or lake view. If there is no natural body of water nearby, a man-made lake or pond will be incorporated in the design if at all possible. A waterfall will be contrived. A reflecting pool will be incorporated. A stream will be diverted or dammed. And the people who live there or come to visit will congregate near the water, always facing it, watching it, mysteriously in thrall.

Poets say this is because we, as all living things, came from the sea. Every body of water is a miniature sea, reminding us of our lost Eden. The sea in any of its replicated forms stirs cellular memories of the ancient time when we swam together in the primordial soup. Bodies of water beckon us to the cradle, endlessly rocking.

The sight of water reminds our DNA that it must constantly reproduce microscopic oceans in every cell of our bodies. The oceans must comprise so much sodium, zinc and phosphate, so much hydrogen, oxygen and nitrogen. They must be ever flowing, with miniature currents and tides waxing and waning. The oceans must cover and nourish all, leaving no dry areas, not even the fingernails or strands of hair. The oceans must claim all, as it was in the beginning, is now and ever shall be.

These tiny, cellular seas are our life support systems in an alien environment as surely as was Neil Armstrong's space suit when he walked on the moon. The DNA must assure an environment for each cell in which it can survive, even while the living body plods along concrete sidewalks or through cornfields, always surrounded by drying air, alternately scorched by sunlight or chilled by ice storms. Through it all, we swim in our warm ocean. We still breathe through water on the surface of our lungs. Our brains work in electrolytic sea currents. Our muscles and bones still move sinuously through that primal ocean, now internalized and miniaturized, but an ocean still.

No wonder the sight of water mesmerizes us. It is the palpable, tangible stuff of which all life is made, from which it came, to which it returns. We don't move from dust to dust. We move from ocean to ocean, through unending ocean. Our bodies know. Our brain stems remember. So we stare at water helplessly and without knowing why, but with some huge and growing sense of calm. Tranquility is knowing one belongs to all of creation and all of the cosmos, without beginning or end. Tranquility flows from the sound of water only.

— July 17, 1983

Spiderman's decision was very important, too

He was about four or five years old, dressed in the uniform of his rank: Tiny, imitation Adidas, Spiderman T-shirt, baby blue jeans and a sober look. He was inspecting the candy display at a drug store. "Make up your mind," said what I assumed to be his mother.

I watched his eyes sweep from the Milk Duds over Hersheys and Baby Ruths to M&M's and Mounds. "Hurry up," said Mom. "We have to go." The eye movements quickened and the hint of a frown appeared on the small forehead.

Mom reached for M&M's. "Take these," she said. "WAIT!" he wailed. "Well, what?" she said. He was still into rapid eye sweeps. "We'll take this," Mom said forcefully.

She snatched up the bag of M&M's, pushed it in the general direction of Spiderman and simultaneously deposited change on the counter. They were out the door in a muffle of small boy protests and big momma assurances that, "You like these. We haven't got any more time to waste. Dad's waiting."

It was a minor drama with no hero and no villain. There had been a crisis, however, and a denouement. It all served to remind me that decision-making for human beings is always difficult, important and personal. It cannot be done satisfactorily by another person, and it can't be rushed. We all need lots of practice and the sooner we begin the sooner we get good at it.

I figured Spiderman's decision was, for him at the moment, just as important as his mother's decision might have been had she been standing in front of a counter at Tiffany's trying to decide between a half-dozen diamond bracelets. I wondered with what good grace Mom might have accepted someone else saying, "We'll take this one. You'll like it. We haven't any more time to waste." WAIT! You betcha, wait — for just as long as it takes. Don't stomp on my flowers!

Small children really have few choices offered them, when you think about it. Someone else decides what they'll wear and eat, when they'll sleep, where they'll play and with what or whom.

This can go on for an amazingly long time, sometimes an entire lifetime. The decisive parent role is taken over successively by teachers, friends, spouses, bosses and finally by the now-grown children of the now-elderly parent.

Whenever I meet a wishy-washy, indecisive person, I wonder about the child he or she was. How many choices? How much rushing the process? How many triumphs or failures of decision? How often was a decision made for this person by someone else?

When Chuck and Jim, the McWhirter twins, were pre-schoolers, I dressed them identically because it was fun, for me. It confused the neighbors and grandparents. The boys seemed uninterested in clothes anyway.

The night before their first day of kindergarten, I suggested these two decide what they would wear to school in the morning. We would have the duds handy to expedite the dash for the bus.

"Blue pants, yellow shirt," said Price. "Gray pants, red shirt," said Pride. "Make up your minds," said Mom. "We HAVE!" said the outraged duo. Of course. They have never dressed identically since.

I had a great deal of decision training at a tender age. Grandmother, the Tyrant, was especially good at it. She had two favorite exercises. One involved a bakery a couple of blocks from her house.

About once a week she handed me an appropriate amount of money and sent me off to the bakery for a half-dozen rolls. Sometimes it was cookies or cupcakes or breakfast rolls. It was always something involving choices. "Please get an assortment," she said. "What's an assortment?" "Many different kinds, but only six in all." "Oh. OK."

It was an important assignment and I could string it out into an hour's work. I pondered everything in the case endlessly. What did I like; what did the Tyrant and Granddad like? Should I get two of only three kinds or four of one kind and two of another? Decisions, decisions. I felt very decisive in that bakery. My mission was important to the family; the choices were mine. The baker probably considered me a pest. I don't remember that; I don't remember taking any criticism at home for my selections, either. I do remember once eating a jelly-filled doughnut with vegetable soup and deciding that had not been a good idea.

The Tyrant's other trick, even more diabolical, was designed to get me out from underfoot for an even longer period of time. She sent me off to a nearby variety store, ostensibly to fetch her a new thimble or spool of thread. It was always a thimble or spool of thread. The trick was to give me an extra 50 cents and say, "While you are there, you might like to buy some new materials for your project."

The project was a hunk of cloth (my choice from the ragbag) installed inside an embroidery hoop. To this I stitched and variously affixed buttons, ribbon snips, bits of colored yarn and all manner of trivia. I considered a project abstract expressionism. I completed many of them, none of which hangs in a house, let alone a museum. No matter. It was fun.

With 50 cents, I could spend a rainy afternoon at the variety store. I could buy a piece of ribbon for a nickel and a button for a dime. There were sequins and fake jewel trims, glitter bits, laces and embroidery yarns. I had to torture myself deciding between this and that and keeping track of pennies. Sometimes the clerk would give me something free, such as the last two inches on a ribbon spool. It was heaven. Cheating and shoplifting had not been invented yet.

What I am trying to illustrate is that the more opportunities we give a small child to exercise choice and practice small, seemingly unimportant, insignificant decision-making, the stronger and more able to manage larger decisions he or she becomes.

I wish Spiderman's mother had permitted him an extra minute or 20 to decide on his candy and had done it with patience and good humor. I am going to tuck the Tyrant's ploys away in my memory box for updating and remodeling on the outside chance Price, Pride or Shampoo Sue (their sister) ever produces progeny for me to grandmother. That'll be the day.

— Aug. 20, 1978

A jolly grandfather won't be around forever

There is a little boy I heard about recently who is haunting me. I've never met him and I don't know his name. I know he's about 12 years old and lives in our town. I heard about this kid through a friend.

A psychologist was assigned to test and talk with this boy in an attempt to find out what, if anything, is bugging him. He is not doing well in school and he's sort of mopey and withdrawn. He hasn't gotten into any heavy trouble that I know of. He's just generally miserable. That's called depression.

The psychologist did whatever psychologists do and could find no horrors of any magnitude except these: The boy's parents are busy, busy, busy. They are not openly affectionate with their son. They love him, however, and they don't abuse or neglect him in any conventional sense. They have him enrolled in a good, no-nonsense, religious school.

The parents' general attitude is that they will take care of housing, food, clothing and other necessities for this boy. The school ought to teach religion, discipline and manners, plus the standard academic subjects. Beyond that, the child ought to be self-sufficient enough to find wholesome amusements and activities. The result ought to be contentment and happiness for all. QED. This is a sort of syllogistic approach to family living.

Unfortunately, it isn't working. The boy has taken to spending most of his free time in a cemetery. It doesn't take big brains to figure out there's something strange about that.

It isn't that he romps around the cemetery with his friends, playing hide-and-seek or let's-scare-ourselves games. That would not be strange. Children with cemetery access often do that as an exercise in imagination and a flirt with the still vague concept of death and afterlife.

This child, however, goes there alone and sits quietly beside the grave of his grandfather. He doesn't bother anybody or anything. He just hangs around by himself, for hours.

His grandfather died some time ago. Before that he used to have fun with the old gentleman. He said he loved his grandfather and knew he was loved back. He can't get any closer than the grave site anymore, so he just hangs around. That's all.

And that's all to this story, so far. You see why it is a haunt. It has no resolution, no ending. It has no melodramatic villain, just a victim, quietly suffering.

One hopes that by now the shrink has advised the parents, the school and all the ships at sea concerning the love deprivation and loneliness of this child. One wonders, at the same time, if it will make any significant difference.

Can a parent who has never done it before learn to hug and snuggle unself-consciously? If easy affection has never come naturally, how does Dad begin? If time together with her child has always been hollow, with what does Mom fill that time today?

We hear and read a lot about parents who knock their children around, starve them, force them to live in filth or otherwise abuse them physically and emotionally. It is vogue to think of such parental abuse taking place in shacks and ghetto apartments, perpetrated by people of few resources and dim intelligence. Poor people, dumb people, rotten, mean, selfish, stupid, scared people who don't know anything about anything. Sometimes that is true.

Sometimes, however, the very models of middle- or upper-class respectability exhibit identical behavior. More often these privileged abusers employ the subtle and destructive mind-bender of which the boy in the cemetery is a victim. They simply withhold themselves and their love from their child.

It is a killer. It's slow and it leaves no bruises. It's hard to spot since the schools, clothes, bicycles, summer camps and other trimmings seem to be evidence of parental love.

I knew one such kid who had his own new car and private apartment in the family manse by age 16. He had been everywhere and done just about everything. His parents went their way and he went his in very well-mannered cadence. He jumped off a water tower to his death at age 17.

I knew another one who told me once about his most memorable Christmas. He was about 10 years old and came home on a train from a private boarding school in the East. He was met at the station by the family car and driver. At home there was a note from "Mumsey." It said she and "Daddy" had gone to the Bahamas for the holiday to escape the terrible winter. There would not be time for him to join them. But never mind. His presents were in a closet. He was to ask the cook for anything at all he wanted for Christmas dinner and, if he chose, the driver would take him round to see all his chums on Christmas Day. Love, love, love, Mumsey.

The victim of this velvet abuse was 33 years old when he told me about it. He wept. (He had become very much the same kind of invisible parent, by the way.)

People who cannot hug and snuggle and enjoy time spent with children are well-advised not to conceive and bear them. Kids aren't decorative accents or historic testaments to the normal sexual functioning of their parents. They are much more than that.

You cannot produce decent human beings without having a rollicking good time with them now and then and providing them with lots of strokes, pats, smooches, conversation and smiles in between times. You most certainly can't pay to have all this done. Not in America. Not anymore. And you cannot always depend on having a jolly grandfather around either. Sometimes they have to leave unexpectedly before the job is done.

— April 8, 1979

The prize at the end is disappointment

I'll call him Walter. He was maybe 60 years old when I got to know him, and miserable.

Walt was one of those guys who hates his job, distrusts his boss, dislikes his associates, can't abide his neighbors, figures he's being victimized by the stores, banks and public utilities and getting absolutely no service from the departments of public works, sanitation, police, fire, and parks and recreation. Walt was reasonably well satisfied with his wife, as far as I could tell. That was it. He fascinated me.

I kept wondering how a presumably normal human being could begin life all pink and grinning and turn into a Walter after only 60 years. I decided to try to find out.

I never did, completely, but I found out one thing about Walt and the way he lived that is a clue. I think.

Walt was very heavy into deferred gratification. It was his lifestyle. The trouble was he deferred so much and so long that he rarely got to the gratification part. When he did, it was always a disappointment.

I'll give you some examples.

Walt had a junky car when I met him. He was always patching it up himself or hiring it done and then complaining about auto repair ripoffs. I asked him why he didn't get a new car. He planned to, he said, next fall, when the dealer closeouts began. "You'll have to put up with this thing through another winter," I said. "I'll get a better deal on the new one," he said.

All winter Walt talked about the new car he was going to buy and cursed the old one. Finally, in late August the next year, he got the new car. He hated it. It was green. He didn't like green. It didn't have some of the options he wanted. It was a dealer closeout.

"Someday, someday . . . " Walt said. Someday he'd have exactly the car he wanted. Phooey, thought I. Never.

Another thing about Walter. He wore terrible clothes. His suits didn't fit well. He always looked rumpled and cheap. He was forever telling me about little discount stores where you could buy shoes for "half what you pay for them at Hudson's" and suits or coats "at wholesale."

Walter earned a comfortable living. Once I asked him why he was so preoccupied with saving a buck here and 50 cents there. He told me:

"Mary and I are buying this chunk of land in Mexico," he said. Mary was his wife. "It's about 20 miles from Acapulco. Beautiful. We're going to build a little house on it and live down there when I retire. We have it all planned. We figure with my pension and what we have saved, we'll be able to have a ball. HAVE A BALL!"

I asked him if he and Mary went to Mexico often. No. They were saving money. I asked him if he had considered retiring early, to enjoy this heaven-on-earth sooner. No. He wasn't going to be cheated out of some pension.

I asked him what he would do in Mexico. He talked about fishing and reading books and sitting in the sun. He said there was a village nearby and he had gotten to know a few of the people. He liked them. He didn't mention anything special or anything he couldn't have done right at home — except look at the ocean and keep warm all year long.

When he talked about it, though, Walt's eyes sparkled and you could tell that this patch of Mexico countryside represented paradise to him — deferred, but shimmering out there close enough to be worth every sacrifice and every deprivation for years and years.

Walter died two years short of retirement. He had a coronary something-or-other and that was that. I don't know what happened to the Mexican property. Maybe Mary sold it; maybe she's down there now. I doubt it.

In a way, I was glad Walt never made it to his dream. I feel certain he would have been bitterly disappointed. Just like the green car, he would have discovered that there wasn't enough water or there were too many bugs or the villagers weren't so pleasant after all.

I am terribly sorry that Walt didn't have more fun with his life along the way. I believe in dreams, and striving and sacrificing to reach them, but this process can be very dangerous.

It's the deferring business that's the problem. We tend to defer the lesser opportunities of the day and year in favor of the greater opportunities we envision coming up tomorrow and "when we retire." Sometimes it's when we can afford it, when I'm older, when I move, when I'm married, when I'm divorced, when, when, when.

In so doing, we defer our lives. This is not only a tragic waste, it makes us angry and bitter. If we make it to the fancied paradise, it is somehow never as wonderful as we expected. This is at least partly because we have all these unconscious resentments about the pleasures and lesser dreams we gave up to get there.

We delude ourselves if we say we really don't mind sacrificing present pleasure for future pleasure, or benefit, or whatever. We do mind. Too much deferring carried on too long, too much sacrifice or self-indulgence turns us to vinegar. It turns the prize at the end into disappointment.

I know that some of this deferred gratification is necessary, even helpful and healthy. We just need to watch the time frames carefully. Otherwise we end up like Walt — cheated, bitter, with a dumb green car and a ticket to the playground. Too late, much too late.

— Sept. 30, 1977

No time for an old sergeant, no time for a fond farewell

Good decent human beings deserve our thanks and appreciation. Sam Blotchek, age 61, is a good, decent human being. Blotchek is not his name; it's what I'll call him. And I'll tell you his story.

Forty years ago, when he was a young man convinced he was needed and would live forever, Blotchek enlisted in the Marine Corps. World War II had begun. Blotchek fought in the Pacific theater with the 1st Marine Division, and by the time the war was over, he had made master sergeant.

Back home, he got a job in an auto plant and joined the Marine Corps active reserve. In 1951, the Korean war erupted, and Master Sgt. Sam Blotchek was recalled. He fought those inglorious Korean battles when he was a little older and a little less sure he would live forever. But he endured and gave an excellent accounting of himself.

After the fighting, Blotchek came back to his job. For 35 years, running a little late and a little short on formal education, Blotchek worked diligently in the same plant. He was promoted to foreman and to various supervisory jobs. He was liked by the workers and by management. Life was good; he was making his way.

In February 1979, a doctor said Blotchek's heart was in bad shape. Clogged arteries, coronary heart disease — Blotchek needed triple bypass surgery. So, he was placed on medical leave, and the surgery was accomplished.

He was making a good recovery until six months ago, when other symptoms appeared. This time the doctors discovered lung cancer. Blotchek underwent surgery again, last June. He is recovering well from this second medical catastrophe, too, but there has been a more recent, painful crisis in his life.

When employes at Blotchek's plant complete 35 years' service, it is tradition that the plant manager, the general foreman, some of the supervisors and some of the men gather for a little celebration. The company gives the 35-year employe a wristwatch. There is a cake. There are short speeches, handshakes, pictures taken. Sam Blotchek's 35-year anniversary was Sept. 17. He wanted that ceremony.

He waited at home for a phone call inviting him to his party. It didn't come. In late November, he phoned the company personnel office to ask if it would be OK for him to appear five days later, on Dec. 4 to pick up some money still owed him. Maybe that would be a good time for the watch presentation ceremony as well. "Oh, yes, of course," said the someone at the other end of the line.

Sam Blotchek thought about how good it would be. It wasn't the watch so much. It was shaking hands with the plant manager and having him and the other men tell him he had been appreciated these past 35 years.

When Blotchek arrived at the plant personnel office, a woman young enough to be his own daughter — young enough to have no idea what it is to fight two wars, work in a factory for 35 years, suffer two major surgeries in order to fight two killer diseases — smiled. She handed Blotchek a check for the money owed him. She went into another room and returned in a few minutes with a box. "And here's your watch," she said, handing it to him.

For Sam Blotchek, the words of the young woman were more horrible than the sounds of grenades and shells exploding around him. They were more gut-wrenching than the doctors' voices telling him he had lung cancer and heart disease. After that one devastating moment, no embarrassed company explanations could revive what had withered inside the man.

"It wasn't right," says Blotchek now, in a voice made husky by the shouts of war, work and disease. "I wanted to enjoy my mellow years. I always did my best. I participated. I contributed. I thought I was appreciated."

I had to coax the story out of Blotchek. "I don't want to get anybody in trouble," he said.

Maybe there is still time for some of his co-workers and bosses to do something decent for Sam Blotchek. You people know who you are, and who he is. Merry Christmas.

— Dec. 11, 1981

It's mighty close to 24-karat freedom

People who complain about living alone make me cranky. Living alone is one of life's genuine luxuries. Those who find themselves in this Brahmin castle ought to walk tall with constant, contented smiles. Do they? Hardly ever.

I was talking with a recently divorced man a couple of weeks ago. He's living alone for the first time in his life, and he's miserable. No wonder.

He's got a kitchen full of Hamburger Helper boxes and Campbell's soup cans. Bright fellow that he is, he can't figure out how to get his socks washed without a wife. His living room is strung with hand-me-down curtains that don't fit the windows and furnished with a couple of folding camp chairs in which he sits a lot, reading Playboy magazine and complaining about his wretched state.

I am told this adult male's widowed mother has now agreed to come in a couple times a week to wash, iron, cook and generally help her baby cope. This mother is making a terrible mistake, but neither she nor her son is likely to listen to me.

This guy reminds me of Charlie Rimes, whom I knew in college and kept track of for a while afterward. Charlie had a job that took him traveling variously in the world.

To my knowledge he had the digestive apparatus of a goat, but Charlie was convinced that foreign food would do him in. Except at home, he lived on grilled cheese sandwiches. Paris, Vienna, Buenos Aires, nothing but grilled cheese sandwiches.

I used to fantasize that Charlie created an international crisis by inadvertently murdering an Eastern potentate. In this fantasy the Maharaja of Pookadoo offers Charlie oranges swimming in rose water as a light refreshment during sensitive negotiations for the camel dung rights in Pookadoo. Charlie demands yak cheese and unleavened bread grilled in lamb fat instead, the very thought of which gives the potentate instant, terminal dyspepsia.

Charlie hated traveling.

Lots of people who find themselves living alone approach life as Charlie approached mealtime — scared. They end up living like that other guy — lazy and wallowing in self-pity. Too bad.

Unfamiliar territory can be very exciting to explore. It is not automatically hostile. Living without accommodating others or being accommodated by them is as close to 24-karat freedom as we get.

People tend to equate living alone with loneliness. Loneliness is a sad state of mind and body and something I certainly do not recommend. It has nothing at all to do with living alone, however. It just means you don't have any friend or friends or other people around whom you enjoy and who enjoy you. That can happen to anybody, anywhere. Married, single, living in a commune or a mansion or a rented room, a person can be lonely if he or she lets it happen.

Living alone is different. It's a priceless opportunity for self-indulgence, above criticism.

You don't have to eat pot roast when you're hungry for apples and cheese. If you fancy purple walls and a black ceiling, silver wallpaper and a green bedspread, you can have them, and ought to. No arguments; no compromises.

You can use ALL the hot water, anytime you want. You can sleep until noon on Saturday if you want to, and nobody will be rattling around telling you it's time to be up and at 'em. (My father used to say that.) You can do the laundry at midnight, if you like, and listen to the Sinatra records at breakfast, if you decide to have breakfast. Maybe you'll have it in bed, with the New York Times.

You do not have to watch the reruns of Baretta or the Monday night ball game, unless you want to. If you want to, you don't have to ask anybody if they mind.

You can be as grouchy or as jolly as you feel like being without making excuses. When you want company, you can invite someone to join you. But you don't have to ask anybody. You have choices, which are your own choices.

Is this not a truly luxurious way to live? Why, then, do people who find themselves alone for any reason sit around and mope? Scared, I figure.

That guy with the Hamburger Helper boxes would rather have crab Louis for dinner, and he could. All he needs is a cookbook and a few pots and pans. He's got plenty of time. He could be a latent Escoffier and he could be having some good, solitary fun exploring the possibility. Learning something new; finding out about his own wonderfulness.

He needn't be solitary either. He could buy a bottle of wine and invite a friend of either sex — he's probably got one or two — to help him scarf down the experiments. He probably won't. Scared as a rabbit. That really does make me cranky.

— July 13, 1977

The uniform and toaster — they were worth saving

The old man walked into an insurance office and inquired about purchasing renters' coverage for the contents of his apartment. He was referred to a salesperson. (I am not sure what insurance sellers call themselves.)

The old man was clean and decently dressed in well-worn clothes. He explained he lives in a neighborhood that has lots of robberies and burglaries. His home is a small apartment in a big building. Everything he owns is there. He thought he should buy some insurance, just in case.

"How much?" — or words to that effect — said the salesperson.

"Let's see," said the old man. "I have a toaster. That must be worth $14 or $15. And there's my old Army uniform. Don't know what that's worth, but I sure would hate to lose it. A portable radio . . ." He went on to name odds and ends. He concluded with a hint of pride, "I've got maybe $600 worth of stuff altogether."

The salesperson smiled. As gently as possible, he told the old man it would be impossible for him to buy insurance on a mere $600 worth of household and personal belongings. It turns out that society and the Amalgamated Insurance Underwriters of the World consider $600 worth of possessions about as insurance-worthy as dust curls under the bed.

The old man shrugged, said he understood, and left. The insurance seller told me about this sometime later.

"It's sad, isn't it?" says he. "Here is an old man with his life nearly done, and everything he owns in the world is worth maybe $600. Hell, some people own one TV set worth $600. The things he mentions that are most valuable to him are a toaster and an old Army uniform."

"It is more mysterious than sad," I say. "I wonder what sort of person he was when the Army uniform was new. I wonder what things he hoped to accomplish and if he ever succeeded. I wonder how he got from being a young man in that uniform to being an old man with next to nothing, except that uniform. What happened along the way? Mostly, how come he still has the uniform? It seems a strange possession to hang onto when everything else goes down the pipe."

Perhaps possessions have little worth or meaning after all, just as the church tells us. Or perhaps the worth fluctuates on some mystical level. I wonder what each of us might save and cherish of all the belongings, baubles and trappings of glory with which we surround ourselves — if we had to choose only one or two things.

If e.e. cummings' much-of-a-wind blew out of the West one day, ripping everything apart, blowing most of it away . . . if the voice of doomsday whispered to each of us that we were not to fear any loss of life, neither ours, nor our loved ones . . . if it said that we would be left with sufficient serviceable clothing (albeit without St. Laurent labels), shelter and beds, food and water . . . if it said that money would no longer have any commercial value whatsoever . . . but told us we might each retain two things from among our existing store of possessions . . . what would they be?

I think I could live without my bicycle and even that silly mirror over my dining room table for which I searched the better part of a year. The stereo, TVs and myriad electric gadgets would not be given a nod, especially not the toaster. Jewelry? Piffle. Cars? Phooey.

Grandfather's chicken picture would be one of my choices. It is an oil painting done by an artist friend of Granddad many years ago. Some gloriously plumed breed of chickens that Granddad raised on a little farm in southern Illinois are the central subject of this work, which probably has a present market value of about $5, tops. No matter. It is a very beautiful painting to me because it evokes Grandfather and many happy memories. The chicken picture would have to be saved.

Beyond that, I'm not sure. Snapshots, perhaps. Books are a definite maybe. So is my guitar — although it is quite true, as my friends blab all over town, that I do not know how to play my guitar and only take it out of its case every once in a while to tune it and decide whether it is yet time to learn to play. So far it hasn't been time. Maybe if everything got blown away, it would be time. Probably.

I think I understand the man and his Army uniform. If things get chipped away little by little and choices of essentials must be made, values change drastically. The $195 Charles Jourdan shoes (which hurt your feet anyway) will go long before the comfortable boots that keep your feet warm and dry in winter. And an old Army uniform — full of memories of youth and dreams, a time of hope and striving, friendships, love, energy, coming through hard times, laughter and sorrow, too — could become a very valuable possession.

— Sept. 29, 1980

A sad situation for mommas and Sallys

I'll call her Sally. She's 25 years old. She lives with a man and plans to marry him later this year. He's happy; she's happy. Sally's mother, however, is miserable and doing everything possible to spread the disease.

Sally got a note from Mom recently. It comprised a log of telephone calls placed by Sally to her mother since January. There were six. This maternal record keeper carefully noted the dates of the calls — about one per month — plus the number of minutes spent in conversation during each. The average was 12 minutes.

This seemed an admirable filial score to me, especially since Sally has several sisters, but the Big M was displeased.

Mom noted that, in addition to the six calls, she had received "only" seven letters in the past seven months, and one — count it — one personal visit from her daughter.

"What's the matter," concludes this paragon of motherhood in her parting, cheap shot. "Don't you like us moral people anymore?"

Sally says her mother makes her feel guilty. She doesn't like the feeling. She wonders how to handle this.

She is asking the wrong person. I wouldn't handle it gracefully. I would consider putting ground glass in Mom's soup. I can't imagine a jury of my peers anywhere in the land convicting me of anything more than disorderly conduct. I don't think I'd actually do it, however. Too unimaginative.

I would probably dial Mom up and say, "You old darlin' you. I got your little note. Why didn't you just say I was a pest with my silly old phone calls and letters? You subtle, sweet thing. You didn't want to hurt my feelings, I know. You didn't want to tell me to stop bugging you with those monthly calls and letters, so you wrote me that cutesy note pretending you want more. Aren't you the lovable one!

"Well, Mom, I don't need the sky to fall. I promise I won't call anymore, and I'll just send you a note a couple of times a year with my current address. Bob and I have been chosen Mr. and Ms. Missionary America, by the way, and we're off to convert the Philistines in Philistia. Decidedly difficult work, that. Send money.

Nice talking with you this last time. Toodles."

Mothers like Sally's get no sympathy from me.

If you're not lovable, why should anybody love you? If you are insulting, demanding, grouchy, whiny, critical and full of complaints — who, but a masochist, wants to spend 10 minutes in your company? It doesn't matter that your name is mother.

I know a whole bunch of moms like Sally's. They are joy suppressors. They take the fun out of everything.

It seems to bug them that the world can twirl for their children without any help from them. I think they must be very insecure women, with poor self-images.

Their theory, apparently is that their kids owe them something — attention — to settle some ancient score. This is never defined and there is never enough attention, but the more of it Mom can squeeze out of her younguns, the more public evidence there is that she is a worthy human being.

I am always amazed at the Sallys of the world who permit themselves to be so victimized. I figure it's a reflex action.

When they were kids and Mom told them they had to eat dinner at home every Sunday and help with the chores and otherwise knuckle under to parental authority, they did it. That's OK. They had no choice.

When they are grown-ups, with choices, Mom still thinks she has a right to jerk the chain, which is untrue. And the reflex makes the kids jump, or feel guilty if they don't. This is silly.

It is also very sad for both the moms and the Sallys. There is never enough attention to suit Mom. There is always more demanded than the Sallys can give. Everybody sinks into a purple funk.

I think people should get together and keep in touch when and if they enjoy it, and only then. Relatives included. And we should treat our relatives as we would our friends or neighbors.

Sally's mother wouldn't dream of logging phone calls from a friend and then scolding the friend because the calls were infrequent or brief. She wouldn't dream of criticizing her friend's lifestyle, if she hoped to keep the friend.

I think Sally ought to hint to Mom that she could lose a daughter the same way. That isn't cruel. It's sensible. It's healthy. For more sad people than we dream, "Momma" is not a funny comic strip.

— *Aug. 8, 1977*

If the kids want to divorce, leave this mother out of it

The man is a decent sort, not prone to attacks of the crazies. He is loyal to his wife, loves his kids, works hard, meets all his obligations handily and wants a divorce.

At last he has been thinking more and more about a divorce lately. He offers up this secret casually and places it on the table for inspection. "It must be male menopause or the mid-life crisis," he says. "I've read about those things. Do you think that's it?"

How should I know?

I look at this fellow, who is no more than an acquaintance, and wonder why he is telling me about his personal torment. Maybe it is because he can't tell anybody who is really close to him. I am a relatively safe sounding board. I will say whatever I say and wander off in some other direction. I may never see him again. If I do, it may be just a smile and a wave in some restaurant. I won't tell his wife. I won't blab his secret all around his neighborhood.

I am thinking about how strange it is that people sometimes tell near-strangers what they should really tell their wives or husbands or best friends.

"Why do you think you want a divorce?" I ask him.

He enumerates a few minor complaints, nothing cataclysmic. It seems to be that he feels generally unloved and unappreciated. There is lack of warmth and stroking in his marriage. I suspect there is much more to it than that, and that he is deeply angry and resentful for these real or imagined slights. I suspect he doesn't know how angry he is. He denies being angry at all.

Why am I listening to this? I am not the Red Cross.

"I couldn't get a divorce anyway," he says. "It's probably silly even to think about it."

"I don't understand that part," I tell him. "It gets easier and easier. Even the Catholic Church has softened its position. Are you afraid you would be wiped out by a divorce, impoverished? You probably have some vision of yourself living in a third-floor, cold-water, walk-up flat with bare light bulbs hanging from the ceilings and cockroaches running races on the walls. Lots of men have that vision. It never materializes."

"It's not the money," he says. "It's my mother mostly. It would break her heart. Just destroy her."

"That is the damndest thing I've ever heard," I say. "You have no idea how your mother might respond. She might not even be surprised. You can't possibly know. Anyway, what does your mother and her hopes and fears have to do with your life decisions? Do you live to please your mother? Is what she wants to happen in your life more important than what you want to happen?"

He looks troubled. He shakes his head. "It would kill her," he decides. "I just couldn't do it."

OK. I tell him to think that one over a little more honestly. We change the subject. I make a mental note to myself:

Make sure your kids know their lives are their own, not yours. Do not be a mother with an easily broken heart.

My head is still a little dizzy from the conversation with this troubled man, which took place many days ago. I am still amazed that pleasing Mom, or at least not displeasing Mom, could be the basis for a major life decision such as whether to stay married or seek a divorce.

It would be easy to dump on this fellow and say he is inventing excuses. I might have told him that "my son's divorce" has never been listed as cause of death on any mother's death certificate. I might have said that most mothers want happiness for their children, ergo, they are quite willing to accept decisions children make in the pursuit of happiness. This is especially true if the child is 30 years beyond puberty and has otherwise exhibited good sense in the conduct of his life.

Never mind. It is the mothers I am more worried about. I will never be a male in mid-life crisis. I am a mother, however, and someday one or all of my children could be suffering symptoms of the divorce dilemma.

Quite frankly, I do not want the responsibility of participating in such an important decision as whether to stay married or kick it. That's a very tough decision. It doesn't need any extra clutter contributed by close family members.

I would be appalled to think of one of my kids wrestling with this divorce decision, burdened by more than the unavoidable personal confusion and sorrow which just naturally arise from a troubled heart. Never mind Mother! It is not Mother's life in crisis. Mother will handle her life decisions; you handle yours. I count on you to accept mine, and you can count on me to accept yours. We will go on from there with a smile, undiminished mutual love and respect, God willing and the creek don't rise.

I think that's the way adult familial relationships ought to work in crisis situations. We can certainly comfort and advise each other, but life choices ought to be made by each person without any burden of regard for the possible rupture of a mother's heart. Mothers' hearts are supposed to be big, accepting and very tough. Otherwise, they're defective.

— March 26, 1980

Shadows are deceptive ... I don't trust them

Mabel Sheehan is 72 years old and has lived on Orkney Street in north Philadelphia for 25 years. It's a ghetto neighborhood. A couple of years ago Sheehan's husband died and since then this woman, whom neighbors describe as intelligent, sturdy and stubborn, has become reclusive and eccentric. She doesn't bathe often, for one thing, and she lets her long gray hair hang loose to her shoulders. She stays in her house most of the time and police say the house is full of trash, junk, garbage and bugs. "I know I'm dirty. I could be clean if I wanted to, but I don't want to," she told a neighbor.

Her eccentricity has drawn attention to Mabel Sheehan and, not surprisingly in her neighborhood, the attention has spawned imaginings and the imaginings have centered on money — which is what no one has enough of on Orkney Street. First, the rumor was that Sheehan had $4,000 or $5,000 squirreled away in her house. Soon it was $45,000 and finally, it was, oh, say $4 million-$5 million or maybe even $45 million!

The trouble began 11 days ago. According to Philadelphia newspaper accounts, the first gang of young toughs broke into Sheehan's two-story brick row house on Thursday, Aug. 24. They ransacked the place as she huddled, terrified, in a corner. Neighbors saw kids run out of the house with handfuls of money. Police say they don't know how much was taken, but Sheehan says she was robbed of $230, the amount of her Social Security check for the month. That, plus an $8-a-month pension, represents her only income.

The Sheehan money rumor spread. It brought thieves back on Friday, Saturday and Sunday. By last Monday the old woman was hysterical, standing in the street, shouting for looters to go inside and "take what you want and be done with it!" The Monday night crowd of onlookers was estimated by police at 300 persons. They gathered to witness or participate in the rape of the widow Sheehan's house. Most of them simply ignored police orders to leave.

Officers so far have arrested 19 persons on charges of illegally entering the house. Eight police officers have been assigned to guard and protect it, plus what few possessions Sheehan has left. The officers say there isn't much left except trash and filth. Certainly, they say, there is no money and probably never was.

Neighbors have offered to clean Sheehan's house and she has been befriended by nuns from a nearby Catholic Social Service Center. A local contractor has volunteered to put iron bars over her windows and doors although he says: "Iron bars won't keep them out if they still think there's money in there."

And they — the swarms of young punks — evidently still think there is. They continue to gather on street corners eyeing the row house and waiting, presumably for the cops to go away.

Sheehan says all she wants is to go back to her home of the past 25 years and live peacefully, albeit as a recluse and eccentric. I don't think she has a dewdrop's chance in hell.

Mabel Sheehan is a victim of her reputation, which was manufactured in the fertile minds of some of her neighbors, but which is as real by now as her name and her address. Mabel Sheehan will forever be branded as a screwy woman, who keeps bags of cash, thousands and thousands of dollars, hidden in and around her house waiting to be stolen. She is the mother lode, the lost treasure of the Incas, a whole garageful of loaded and unguarded Brink's trucks. She is a sitting duck.

Like so many people who become victims of undeserved reputations, this 72-year-old widow will spend the rest of her life running away from it, and wondering how it happened. It is a tragedy rarely considered by most of us in our jousts with the real and tangible demons which present themselves daily.

A girl I knew in high school was said to be "easy." It was in a small town at a time when sexual experimentation was common, but covert. A reputation for promiscuity was loathesome. She had it. I don't know why. I can't remember a single boy or girl who had any first-hand knowledge of this girl's ever making it with anybody, but we all just KNEW she did. She had few friends and almost no dates, which would seem to argue against her alleged nymphet rep, but we didn't consider that. There were rumors, and they followed her to college and beyond. Last I heard she was living with her parents, working at some job or other and still an outcast. She was seeing a shrink.

We all know people who acquire reputations as drinkers, grouches, sexual adventurers, big spenders, tightwads and all manner of other characteristics based on little or no evidence. The reputations become accepted as reality and the persons they attach to are mislabeled, sometimes for life. Sheehan is a recent, dramatic victim.

We each believe what we want to believe, then we act on the beliefs. We seldom act on the reality of a person; sometimes we never know the reality or would reject it if we discovered it. Reputation becomes reality. Shadows become substance. Shadows are deceptive and distorted most of the time. I don't trust them.

— Sept. 3, 1978

Time warped and worn,
with a heart well hidden

His name is not Barney, but that's what I'll call him. He was a night rewrite man at a newspaper when I was a very green reporter. Barney may have been 50 years old then, when all this happened. Fifty is my guess. He could just as easily been 60 or 40. It was impossible to tell.

Barney was time warped and worn. He was a good rewrite man with a foul mouth. He typed and barked questions at the reporters and muttered insults and obscenities, all through swirls of Chesterfield cigaret smoke, which made his eyes squint. He chain-smoked Chesterfields. When Barney wasn't working, he put his feet on his desk and complained to anybody who would listen that the reporters were all slow or stupid or both.

Barney had little patience with reporters of either sex. He taunted them. He thought women reporters were especially useless. It didn't matter how good they were or how much experience they had. He called them all broads, bitches and other less flattering names. He made coarse jokes about them behind their backs. He called one woman the Toad. He called me Girl.

Girl was gentle coming from Barney. It was almost complimentary. I felt flattered, and I liked him. Not many people liked him, because he was cynical and mean. He was also mysterious.

I asked an editor about him. The editor said Barney had been a whiz kid reporter in the 1920s — young, aggressive, smart. He ran with a crowd of semi-hoods and show girls, all hard-drinking, big-spending types. He had lots of powerful friends and informers. Whenever there was a shoot-up, a bust or a killing, Barney knew it was coming down before it did. He was there. He could talk to both sides. He wrote wonderful stories.

Barney's glory years, as glorious as they got, were finished before I met him. By then, he was living from paycheck to paycheck, seemingly without friends and without caring to have any. Sometimes he drank with hookers. Otherwise, he drank alone.

I was in Phoenix, Ariz., at a party. It was in a beautiful house perched on the side of a mountain overlooking the lights of the city.

The guests wore dinner clothes. They had come mostly from the Phoenix-Scottsdale area as well as California and New York. The party had nothing to do with newspapers.

I found myself talking with a beautiful woman in a long, white gown and major jewelry. I mentioned Detroit, and her eyes grew large and lively. I mentioned the newspaper, and she smiled.

"Tell me," she said. "Do you know Barney . . . ?" She mentioned his last name. "What sort of editor is he now? Is he running the paper?"

"Not exactly," I said. I told her he was writing, which was true.

"He was always such a fine writer," she said. Her eyes sparkled. "And such a kind, loving man. So intelligent. Brilliant really."

I asked how she knew him. She told me they had met when she was very young, and working as a dancer in some sleazy Detroit nightclub. Barney had befriended her. He had given her money and helped her family. He had encouraged her to finish high school and stay away from pimps. When she told him she loved him, he told her he loved her, too, but that she should grow up some more. She promised to do that. They laughed about it.

"He was so handsome," she said, "with those beautiful blue eyes and the blond curly hair. Is he still handsome? Is he happy? Is he married?"

"Very handsome," I lied. "Not married. I don't know about happy."

She told me that when she left Detroit Barney had staked her to a month in Las Vegas to look for a dancing job. She found one, then another. She found a husband. They had been married for many years. The husband died. She was now financially secure, living in Phoenix, selling commercial real estate. She owned her own company.

"Will you give Barney something for me?" she asked, bubbling, almost like a school girl again. Of course I would.

She wrote something on the back of one of her calling cards. The message meant nothing to me, a few words, some code between old lovers. I took it home to Barney.

I handed it to him at the beginning of his night shift. I told him about the party. He stared at the card.

"She is very beautiful," I told him. Barney said nothing. "She loves you, or did, and wants to love you again. She wants you to phone her. She wants very much to see you. She asked all about you, everything."

Barney's head jerked up, and he stared hard at me. His eyes were blue, and pleading. "What did you tell her?" he asked.

"Everything!" I said. "That you are handsome, charming, talented; that we all love you and couldn't run the paper without you. Just the truth. Are you going to call her?"

Barney ran his fingers over the face of the card twice, then he tossed it in a wastebasket. He lit another Chesterfield and put his feet up on the desk.

I called him a monster and a jerk. He swore at me.

We were pals after that and, once, when I was very sick in the hospital, Barney sent me a get-well card covered with violets. There was a very tender verse after which he wrote, "Jesus can wait. You stay here, Girl." Nobody believed Barney sent it.

— Oct. 26, 1980

Which was the reality and which the dream?

I was aware of his youth first. It screamed out from a skinny boy's body clad in the uniform of the U.S. Army. He looked 16. I guessed he was probably a few years older, but I was reminded of some small boy wearing his favorite Superman T-shirt very proudly, never understanding how laughable the label was on a twerp of a kid.

He was Corporal Somebody, age unknown, preened and polished in his khaki and boots, cap in hand, sitting in his assigned window seat on the plane, heading home to Detroit. God, he was young! He still had acne. The whiskers he had no doubt ritually shaved with his Trac II many hours earlier were beginning to sprout in little tufts here and there. He wasn't even fully feathered, just a fledgling. A man I judged to be pushing 60 eased into the seat next to the corporal. It was cramped and difficult for him to accommodate a spreading behind and a belly that appeared to have been well-fed and watered over more than a half century, but he managed the chore. He and the corporal fell into instant, easy conversation.

"What's your outfit?" the fat man wondered. I didn't hear the answer. Something to do with trucks and supply. The corporal had been stationed in Germany for two years, he told the older man. He liked it. Beautiful country. He liked the Army. Good duty. There began a long conversation about Germany then and now, the Army then and now, and such unshared yet shared experiences between these strangers from different generations.

"Do you get fresh milk?" the older man wanted to know. What a strange question, I thought. What a small thing to wonder about. Yes, fresh milk, the soldier said.

"Did you ever polish your boots with floor wax?" the young man wanted to know. The older one chuckled, shaking his seat along with the lard around his middle. "Johnson's Glo-coat!" he said. The young one said everybody uses the kind with acrylic in it now, layer after layer, until the leather looks like it's under glass.

There was talk of rifle practice. The boy-soldier likes it and called it "fun." He said he did well at that. There was talk of marches and maneuvers, field packs, C rations, passes and leaves in towns and villages, beer halls, dance halls and girls. Not women. Girls.

There was no talk of killing or of battles. The older man never brought it up. The younger man obviously had not thought about battles, let alone experienced one. It was all as if these two had discovered they had attended the same summer camp and now were discussing the games, the counselors, the chores and the excitement of that wonderful experience.

Is it always this way with soldiers? I wondered about that. Is it always the fellowship and the drill which is remembered, never the purpose and the ethic? With so many men the time spent in some unit, some branch of the military service, with some clutch of soldiers or sailors or marines in some godforsaken corner of the world is the time of maximum excitement and importance in their lives.

Never mind that you are separated from home and people who love you. Never mind that you are doing the work of killing or preparing to kill. If that is considered at all, it is put in the perspective of duty and honor, bravery and willing sacrifice for the sake of the folks back home. Sometimes it is even ennobled with the idea that the preparation or the killing itself is necessary to preserve democracy.

I was glad the older man did not regale the younger with accounts of the Normandy landing or the Battle of the Bulge. I kept looking at this young soldier's clear eyes and innocent face, acne and all. I kept seeing the faces of some old marines I know who went through a couple of wars. There is a dramatic difference. I wanted the kindness and gentleness and kid-eagerness of that face to age properly into kind, gentle, alert middle and old age without the experience for which the kid was being prepared and preparing himself.

"It's my folks' wedding anniversary," the soldier said. "I told them I'd be home in late July, see," he said. "But they're having this big 25th wedding anniversary party and all the family is getting together so I asked the CO and he worked it out so I could come home now and surprise them. Boy, are they gonna be surprised!"

They'll cry, I thought. There will be hugs and kisses. The kid will show off his sharpshooter medal and talk about using the floor polish on his boots.

He'll show them all pictures of the German countryside and castles on the Rhine. He'll talk about the beer halls and the girl he met at the country dance where there wasn't any oom-pah-pah, band but a pick-up rock group playing old Beatles tunes instead. He'll tell them about this summer camp experience of his, and they'll be pleased to see he has cut his hair and learned to clean under his fingernails. His dad will fix him an Imperial and Coke to drink. His mother will stuff him with cake. They will be happy together. Then he'll go back.

I observed this soldier and listened to him on a plane headed for Detroit the day after Memorial Day. I realized sometime in the narrative that his journey had begun the day before, while ceremonies of awesome remembrance were taking place at the Tomb of the Unknown Soldier at Arlington National Cemetery and at cemeteries throughout the nation. I wondered which was the reality and which the dream. I have not yet decided.

— June 3, 1979

You can have the lemons, the pats of butter, too

I do so hate to complain, as you all well know. Now and again, however, I lose control. This is one of those nows.

I cannot abide those little dabs of butter stuck on little squares of cardboard and covered with little squares of paper which are served up like a bowl of peanuts in most restaurants. They upset my stomach. Similarly and equally reprehensible are the little dabs of butter wrapped in aluminum foil and the little dabs of butter contained in molded plastic thimbles which have foil lids cemented to their tops.

Restaurateurs of America, get rid of them all! Do it now or I shall be forced to mount a nationwide grass-roots movement dedicated to hanging you all on meat hooks by the seats of your pants — or panties, where applicable.

I know butter is expensive and messy to handle and nobody can afford to waste it. That's your problem and I expect you to deal with it, gracefully. I don't even want to know about it. I've got my own problems with the high cost of capers, which I like to add to butter. Occasionally. At home. Back to the restaurants . . .

All those metal, plastic and paper wrappings create an unsightly mess on the table. What's even worse, since each niggling nibble is individually wrapped it is necessary to make a show of unwrapping it. Unkind companions on starvation diets have been known to count the wrappers and comment. "My, my," they say. "Isn't that the FOURTH pat of butter you are putting on your mashed turnips?" It is bad enough to suffer through a luncheon of watercress and mashed turnips, at $4.95, in order not to be intimidated by food freak friends. It is intolerable to find the restaurateur in cahoots. Have you ever tried to choke down mashed turnips WITHOUT butter? See.

While I'm at it, please get rid of all those other little packets and pouches, the ones filled with a half-teaspoon each of mustard, catsup, mayonnaise, horseradish and I don't know what else. There is never enough of any of that stuff in one packet and always too much in two. You get the stuff all over your hands trying to get just the proper amount on your whatever.

The same goes for sugar and other chemicals in packets. What is a person supposed to do with the leftovers? I always end up with most of the sugar left in the packet. I don't want it. I don't know what to do with it. It spills. I hate it. Whatever happened to sugar bowls with cubes or loose sugar in them? Oh, yes. Get rid of the little plastic thimbles filled with cream, too. Give us a cream pitcher.

If you refuse to do all of the above mentioned, then at the very least please provide every table with a large wastebasket into which we may toss all the plastic and paper and foil and leftover garbage previously encased therein. Thank you very much.

This brings us to the napkin dilemma. It is more a napkin crisis. Heaven knows how many Countess Mara ties and Jonathan Logan polyesters have been ruined for lack of napkins. What we need are either honest-to-Wamsutta woven cloth jobbies or paper imitations larger than postage stamps and sturdier than cobwebs. Take a look at the abominations which presently pass for napkins in most restaurants.

Paper, flimsy and small. Nobody's lap, not even Olive Oyl's, could be covered by a wisp roughly three-by-five-inches wide. Oh, but that's folded double, you say. Certainly, it is. And even folded double this silliness soaks through whenever a thundercloud is sighted over Livonia. If you refuse to provide full-size adult persons with full-size adult napkins, then be warned. I shall demand at least six of the mini-type with every course. Better have that wastebasket handy.

On to lemons. People who take lemon in iced tea are not offended by this. I drink tea plain, or straight, if you prefer. It always comes with this silly wedge of lemon on the tiny plate even when I say, "No lemon, thank you." I don't know what to do with the lemon. Every time I pick up the glass, the lemon just naturally slides down into the middle of the plate. It's in the way. Lemons can tell when you don't like them. I can either swallow the lemon slice or drop it in that wastebasket. Bring me lemons on their own plate (to be ignored) or don't bring me lemons at all. Get it? Got it. Good.

That takes care of just about everything until we order. If we could please have the menu? No menus? Printed on the wall? Printed on the napkin! I wrapped a lemon wedge in it. I think I'll go home and scramble an egg.

— July 17, 1978

Overnight, front and rear go pop! pop! pop!

I am taking tennis lessons. I have played tennis, off and on, better and worse, since I could talk. I know exactly what this tennis instructor is going to tell me, but I am paying good money to hear it all again and to run around a court and sweat and probably develop tennis elbow.

Why am I doing this? Any sensible person might ask. I am doing this to atone for liking Scotch whisky, cigarets, real cream in real coffee, bacon, eggs, butter and assorted other things upon which generations of my ancestors flourished, well into their 90s.

Unfortunately, the staples of Granddad's Good Life have been declared poisonous and hazardous to my health. I could ignore all that, relying on the memory of those healthy old goats and the sure knowledge that tomatoes were once considered poisonous, too. It isn't that easy, however. Most of the good stuff also has been found to accelerate the aging process. This is absolutely shocking news.

To die is still acceptable in contemporary society. To die wrinkled and lumpy, however, is not. This latter happening is considered symptomatic of a serious character flaw. We are all supposed to remain slender, supple and smooth as spring onions, until we are roughly 95 years old. Then it's OK to die of something inorganic. It's OK to be run down by a truck while participating in a bicycle marathon, for example.

I am not at all convinced that anything actually stops, slows or in any way affects the natural aging processing. Guilt alone drives me back to the tennis court. Most of my friends are health and exercise freaks. When I crumble into a heap of dry skin flakes and cholesterol jelly, I don't want them saying, "Tsk. Tsk. She didn't even try." I'll try. A little. It won't help.

I talked about some of this with a friend recently. She agrees with me. "It starts hitting you roughly after the 28th birthday," she says. "It begins with little lines under the eyes. One by one, things begin to go. It always happens overnight. You hop into bed in the prime of your life and when you wake up, CELLULITE!"

"It's so terrible," I say. "Do you think eating alfalfa sprouts would make a difference?"

"No," she says. "I've made quite a study of this. Would you like to know the natural progression? It's pretty grim."

We order a plateful of shoestring potatoes to nibble, and she begins the natural progression:

"After the lines under the eyes, you notice one tiny broken blood vessel on the face. It's from all the liquor you've been consuming regularly for years, of course. It's so depressing, you have to have a drink, immediately.

"Next, all of the beauty articles you have read so smugly over the years — because they certainly didn't apply to you — start to swim before your eyes. Dry hair; dry skin. You dream about them. I once dreamed I had blue legs, completely blue. I woke up and looked for them and they were there, varicose veins!

"Then it's support hose. You fall for that stuff about how these hose massage your legs, but it's really just support for the varicose veins. Before you know it you're into the tummy and fanny holder kind of pantyhose, too. Control top, it's called. The front and rear go, pop! pop! Overnight."

"I'll be afraid to go to bed tonight," I moan. "This is the worst," she says, leaning closer. "It's the upper arms. I do my own windows. I scrub floors. How could my upper arms turn to flab overnight? Well, they did. It's like a 1975 Pinto. Perfect one day; rusted out the next. No more sleeveless dresses!"

I am morose. "That takes care of just about everything," I say.

"Wrong!" she says. "The neck is awful. One day it's smooth. Next day it looks like the lattice crust cherry pie picture in Good Housekeeping. It gets all full of crisscrosses, intersecting lines. Suddenly you're into scarves and turtle necks, for the rest of your life."

"If all of this starts at about age 28, how long does it take to wreak its havoc?" I wonder. "Maybe there's still time to pig out on wheat germ and stand on my head long enough, often enough, to stop the carnage."

"It takes a couple of years. By age 30 your ankles begin to swell in the afternoon."

I tell her there's absolutely no hope for me then, with or without tennis lessons, with or without cigarets and coffee cream.

"Me either," she sighs. "My 30th is coming up. The cruelest time is when you walk into the bathroom in the morning and look at yourself with all these handicaps and it's time to take your birth control pill. Why do it? Who cares? Who would want to spend any time with you? These are supposed to be the happiest, most romantic years of your life and there you are all turned to cellulite."

"Overnight," I say.

"Pop, pop," she says.

Tennis is going to be a waste of time.

— May 21, 1978

If anyone asks, here's why the Empress has no clothes

The reason I don't have a gorgeous wardrobe is that I hate shopping for clothes.

The reason I hate shopping for clothes is that I hate trying them on.

The reason I hate trying them on is that it means I have to go into one of those ditsy dressing rooms, take off most of my clothes and play peekaboo with the saleslady. Or, I have to stand in a big dressing room and play peekaboo with a half-dozen other seminaked shoppers. Don't tell me they aren't looking. I know they're looking.

When you don't like strangers ogling your body (mine is composed entirely of virgin cellulite, except for my fingernails), even the ditsy private dressing rooms are unsatisfactory. That's because the saleslady will never let you take all 20 things you want to try into the room at once. She thinks you're a shoplifter.

She doesn't say so. She says, "I'm Miss Spiffy. We'll just take six of these things in the room now. Call me when you're ready for some of the others or if you need help."

The first thing you do after Miss Spiffy leaves you with the six things you are permitted to have in your solo presence is attempt to close the dressing room curtain. That is impossible.

There is a company somewhere that makes these curtains for women's apparel stores. All the curtains are four inches too narrow for the doorways because the curtain company also thinks we are shoplifters. It figures Miss Spiffy ought to keep an eye on us no matter what.

You tug the curtain to the right and line up its right margin with the right doorjamb. Good. The left margin of the curtain is now fully three inches shy of meeting the left doorjamb. Bad. You have a clear view of three dressing rooms across the hall in which three other women made entirely of cellulite are struggling into and out of various garments with their curtains flapping. Don't look.

You pull your own curtain back and forth, to and fro, shaking and coaxing ripples out of it in a futile attempt to make it cover the doorway. You have spent 15 minutes in this exercise. Miss Spiffy reappears. "How are we doing? Anything I can take out? Shall I bring some of the others in?"

Go away, please, Miss Spiffy. Wait for me to trumpet like an elephant caught in a tar pit. Unless you hear that, leave me alone. All alone. Got it? Good.

There is nothing to do but position the curtain so you can see only two dressing rooms on each side of your curtain. Now, be sure you have unfastened all the buttons and unzipped all the zippers of the garments you wish to try. Look right and left, up and down the hallway. Note that Miss Spiffy is nowhere in sight. Fine. It's now or never!

Disrobe. Toss your clothes in a heap and kick them into a corner. Reach for the first garment you plan to try on. Pull it over your head, getting your right shoulder hopelessly stuck and your left elbow pinned against your ear. (You forgot to unbutton a button, you idiot.) Wiggle. Squirm. Moan. Trumpet!

Freeze as you hear the curtain slide wide open. Listen in horror as you hear Miss Spiffy at your side saying, "How are we doing? Anything I can take out? Shall I bring some of the others in?"

Mumble, "Gromble pulfitz sanamanangit!" as Miss Spiffy helps ease the strangling garment over your head. Stand blushing in near-nakedness. Cower behind the flapping curtain. See a woman with even more cellulite than yourself paddle unashamedly down the hallway wearing nothing but purple bikini panties and major jewelry. She is waving a dress, calling, "Miss Spiffy. Oh, Miss Spiffy. Do you have this one in size 16?"

Dress, go home, pour yourself a stiff Scotch. Riffle through the Brooks Brothers, the Talbots and Horchow's catalogs. Order anything, in four colors. Wonder why modesty is a virtue when it costs so much.

— *Sept. 4, 1981*

'May I help you?' asked the salesperson

We were talking at lunch the other day about how you have to fight your way in and fight your way out of most stores. It isn't just the big department stores anymore. Small specialty shops have caught the disease.

Every aisle is jammed with junk; every counter top is covered with display merchandise. Checkout is supermarket style and product information is scarce. If you corner a salesperson who isn't busy-busy-busy and ask about the passion pink peignoir you saw in the store window, you get a blank stare and an invitation to rummage through the racks of what the salesperson thinks are peignoirs. Some of them turn out to be beach robes. You're on your own, Sister, and good luck!

Four of us, discussing this situation, sigh heavily and I resist the temptation to talk about how the J.L. Hudson Co., before it became Hudson's, used to have salespeople stationed every 15 feet behind gleaming showcases of merchandise, which was all neatly folded and stacked by color and size. And how the salespeople knew the merchandise and could give helpful hints on its care and quality. And how there were also roving salespeople on the floor to wonder, "May I help you?" and even answer questions and solve problems. I bring up none of that. We discuss further.

"The worst part," says one of us, "is that even after you find something you want to buy, you have to toss it over your shoulder and wait in a bus line to pay for it. Then they check your credit card, your driver's license and everything except your blood pressure before they remove those chunks of lead they have stapled to the hems of things and finally put it all in a tissue paper bag, which rips open within 10 minutes if it contains anything heavier than a feather boa."

We sigh heavily and I resist the temptation to talk about the days at Jacobson's when everything was packed in boxes and the salesperson asked, simply, "Cash or charge?" and if you opted for charge, he or she would smile pleasantly and ask that you spell your name and provide your address, please "to help with the billing." If there was any checking of credit, nobody knew. We don't talk about that, but we discuss.

"The thing I hate is having to walk all over the store, up and down to four departments, pawing through stuff and trying to find the right shoes or something just to put together one outfit. The dress is one place, the shoes another, the scarf is two floors away. Lord help you if you need a special bra or slip or piece of jewelry. It can take half a day, and it's no fun at all." She sips a Chablis and sighs. I stop resisting the temptation to talk about what used to be.

"It used to be that you could dial up a favorite salesperson and ask to have a bunch of stuff gathered up and then come in and try it on in about an hour and a half," I say. "You know, dresses, suits, blouses, shoes and accessories all right there, in the fitting room. Your salesperson did the running around before you arrived. It was fun. You told her when you would be in and what you were looking for and she gave you some choices and that was it."

Everybody stops sighing and stares.

"Sure sounds dull," says Lolita.

"And uncreative," says Natasha.

"Intimidating," says Wilhelmina, ordering another Chablis. "How were you sure you weren't being ripped off? How did you know something you liked just as well wasn't on sale? How could you ever say you didn't like any of it after the salesperson went to all that trouble?"

"Yeah?" I say. "Well how about when the good old stores sent you a bill once a month with NO FINANCE CHARGE and if you missed a month they only sent you a friendly letter saying you probably forgot? That was swell. And when they delivered everything?"

"Inhibiting," says Lolita. "I understand back when that was done, you couldn't charge anything more until you paid up. My mother told me that she once had to stay out of Saks for three solid months because she owed them $200 and was afraid they would arrest her if she tried to charge a pair of gloves."

"They would not have arrested her," I tell them.

"What's deliver?" Natasha wants to know.

I sigh heavily. "That's when you buy something and ask the store to deliver it to your house in their truck," I tell her.

"They do that with washers and dryers, but not pantyhose," she says smugly.

"They USED to," I tell her. "Anything at all; even a package of needles and a couple of spools of thread. Listen. Things didn't used to be so awful out there. Wanna hear about floor walkers?"

Everybody is staring at me.

"You are either much older than we suspected or there is something funny in your salad," says Lolita. "What is a floor walker?"

"I forget," say I. "It's just a fantasy. I have lots of fantasies. Please pass the salt."

— *Jan. 23, 1978*

Why not be shocking or droll or naughty?

A man I know telephoned the Oakland County Friend of the Court recently to conduct some sticky divorce-related business and was put on "hold" briefly. During this wait he was serenaded by one of those musical tapes which many organizations employ these days to keep callers semipatient while stranded in electronic limbo.

"Everything was OK," says he, "until all of a sudden this female vocalist starts cooing, 'You don't have to say you love me, just be close at hand . . . you don't have to say forever, I will understand . . .' It was quite a start."

I chuckled. I imagined some country-western type male dressed in tight jeans and a plaid shirt standing in the phone booth calling the Friend of the Court. Suddenly Tammy Wynette would wail in his ear all about how tragic is the "D-I-V-O-R-C-E." He would sob in his RC Cola. Maybe the caller would be a spiffy suburban woman worried about her alimony and she'd hear Englebert pleading, "Please release me, let me gooooo . . . 'cause I don't love you anymooooooo . . . " The brute!

My friend went on to suggest that someone should organize these tapes either to minimize this potential blast effect or to capitalize on it somehow.

I like capitalize better. It would be possible to be shocking or droll or very naughty.

How about if you called the mayor's office, for example, and while waiting on hold you were treated to a medley of "Politics and Poker" plus "A Little Black Box." That's the one in which all the politicians explain their high life-style despite low pay by saying they nickel and dime their lunch money away in a little black . . . never mind, you have to hear it. Too obscure.

"What if you called the IRS," suggests friend, "about an audit, let's say. You're nervous. You're worried. They put you on hold and you hear, 'All of me . . . why not take all of me?' How do you like that?"

We're getting there. "Of course, there are some obvious reasonable choices," I tell him. "The travel agents should play things like

' California Dreamin" and 'April in Paris' or 'Georgia on My Mind.' And the airlines could go with Sinatra singing 'Fly Me to the Moon' or 'Come Fly With Me.' I'm going to have to work on this. It could be fun."

I did and it was. I thought about Edison using "You Light Up My Life" on its telephone hold tape and the gas company utilizing "Light My Fire."

All divorce attorneys ought to incorporate the "Somebody Done Somebody Wrong" song, and it would strike a blow for honesty if lawyers as well as doctors and dentists used Abba's tricky little number, "Money, Money, Money." This is an openly avaricious ditty incorporating the line, "It's a rich man's world." I'll say!

The prosecutor's office could use a telephone tape. "You gotta know when to hold 'em, know when to fold 'em, know when to walk away and know when to run . . . " Maybe the cops would like that one, too.

Massage parlors might use "Witchcraft," what with the icy fingers up and down the spine and all. Car companies do not approve, but they could give callers on hold a chuckle with Johnny Cash's "One Piece at a Time" which has to do with stealing a Cadillac off the assembly line bit by bit.

Obviously Amtrak would use "Chattanooga Choo Choo," "Wabash Cannonball" and assorted train songs, which are numberless.

All the TV newsrooms — which put people on hold interminably — could have a grand medley of "No Business Like Show Business," "Hooray for Hollywood" and "Stairway to the Stars." Stuff like that.

For dating services it is "I Love You Just the Way You Are," "Some Enchanted Evening" and "All Alone By the Telephone." That's easy. I'm stuck for aluminum siding companies and insurance salesmen.

I was tempted to suggest "Everything's Coming Up Roses" for all the funeral directors, but somebody said that was tasteless. I couldn't resist.

— March 11, 1979

Handwriting on a wall tells a sad story

Thy ar eveny. It's scrawled in black paint on a building wall in a particularly miserable part of Detroit. I've been driving past this urban Rosetta stone off and on for more than a year, and every time I see it I try to figure out what the graphic communicator had in mind. What is it, or was it, that he or she thought so important that it should be written indelibly for all the rest of us to read? Thy ar eveny. It makes me very sad to see it.

I don't care that someone painted a message on the wall. The neighborhood is full of them. Oscar dog, ganster (I think that means "gangster") hoodlums, dirty low down honky, BKs ARE ---.

Most of the four-letter words in the English language are there, properly spelled. It's all part of the urban landscape in this neighborhood, and I have often thought that the brightly painted obscenities and the proudly scrawled names — Sweet Baby Lila, Ski Dog Charlie — liven up the crumbling buildings with their boarded over windows and doors. It is a sign of life and spirit.

"Thy ar eveny" is disappointing, however. I think of the person who had the compulsion or desire to tell us something, tried and failed. I think that anyone agile enough to operate a can of spray paint ought to be able to get the message across, even if some of the words are misspelled. And I worry about what is happening to language.

We hear constantly of the failure of our schools, especially inner-city schools, to teach children basic skills. Literacy, the capacity to read and write, has become a subject for discussion and argument instead of instruction. Teachers, parents, kids, administrators, social scientists and tourists from Baltimore, if asked, all have pet theories about why kids can't read and write and whether that's good or bad.

There are those who say it is no longer so important to stress these skills in an age of television, computers and picture-book instruction sheets. There are even those who say that standard English usage is foreign to many ethnic groups, as foreign to their daily experience as Latin or Greek, and we should, therefore, never mind teaching English except as, perhaps, a second language.

Well, balderdash, claptrap and piffle! Somewhere in this city is someone who glommed onto a can of black spray paint and tried to tell me something and it came out "Thy ar eveny," which I can't understand. That, alone, is reason for standard English usage and for teaching everybody how to read and write one language. I can probably live without getting the message, but the graffiti writer has failed. He or she ought to be outraged.

I have a lawyer friend who was assigned to defend a young man accused of a felony. From the witness chair the accused testified that he was "sitten on the do-fold listenin' to the dooley" at the time of the crime. What is a do-fold? What is a dooley? This man's future for the next several years depended, at least in part, on his ability to communicate clearly to the court. It took some time and tortured explanation to discover that the do-fold was a kind of hide-a-bed which "do-fold" to make a couch. The "dooley" was a record player. It had dual speakers, or somesuch.

We are told this is street language. That means it is a tongue understood and routinely used by members of an ethnic group, at least in certain neighborhoods. That's OK with me. When I was a kid, we had our own street language. We called it slang, and so did our parents and teachers. We used it for fun and to confuse our elders and the kids from Dearborn, who had their own street language. All of us also understood English, however, and none of us confused the two.

No teacher or misguided social scientist suggested that the schools or society ought to change the standards of common usage to accommodate our private language and illiteracy.

We now have something called "transformational grammar" being espoused by educators. Transformational grammarians contend it is perfectly OK to split infinitives and use "ain't" for "is not" and "are not," because these practices are common in the spoken language of large numbers of people. Using this example of clear thinking, do-fold and dooley will first be accepted and then normalized in the language taught in ghetto schools, and perhaps taught as part of a foreign language course offered in West Bloomfield schools. Within a generation or two we'll have all the problems a Portuguese citizen today has understanding his native language in Brazil.

Transformational grammar is foolishness. Failure to teach standard English usage — reading and writing — is a cheat. It doesn't cheat me. It cheats the kid who wrote "Thy ar eveny" on a wall and wanted me to understand it. It cheats the young man in the courtroom. These are the people who should be raging against their own inability to read and write and speak a common language. Transformational grammar be damned.

— March 19, 1978

A smart adversary gives some points to the other guy

"You have to let the other guy win some points," he says. He's a lawyer and all they ever talk about is lawyering. This time it's trial strategy, over lunch. I sort of tune out, preferring to poke at my salad and daydream about whether I should go to Crete with Kris Kristofferson or Paul Newman, should such a conflict ever occur in my social calendar. You have to let the other guy win some points. I agree with that. I tune back in.

"If you show the other guy up as wrong in everything, a real no-brainer, he'll never forgive you," says Perry Mason. "Neither will the judge or the jury. If you're smart, you pick the points you can give away and you let him take them. He saves face. The jury figures he had his moments. You still win the case, but the other attorney and his client and the judge and everybody feels better than if you just ripped him apart."

Having so pontificated, this practitioner sits back and puffs his pipe. I forget about Crete for the moment and begin to think maybe not all lawyers have mashed turnips for brains.

I wonder if they teach that stuff in law school or if he figured it out all by himself. I know a lot of people who never figure it out. Pity.

Plaintiffs and defendants certainly aren't restricted to court-rooms. They come in all ages and sizes and places. They are not necessarily well matched for skill or clout, and they don't all understand the rules, or stick to them. Everyone believes his or her cause is just and the arguments are passionate, if not weighty. The more strongly a viewpoint is held, or opposed, the more the parties go for the kill, and this can result in gawdawful battles and decisions. That rule — you have to let the other guy win some points — could save a lot of emotional bloodshed.

Parents make especially poor defendants and plaintiffs. They think they know it all and typically go for unconditional surrender. "Do what I say and don't argue," is a favorite adversary logic employed by parents. I learned that sometimes you can win the case with better effect by letting the other guy, albeit a little one, win some points. I was a newcomer in Mother School at the time.

Son James, the Determined, who had always had the tenacity of Winston Churchill holding the white cliffs of Dover against the Valkyrie, was about four years old at the time. He had discovered matches. He had discovered how to strike matches. He had discovered that striking a match caused it to burn and that a burning match could cause other things to burn. He was delighted by his scientific discoveries, and he was driving me bonkers!

Knowing that this is what kidologists call "age-typical behavior" did absolutely nothing positive for my mental health. I was sure that we would all soon perish and that Mrs. McWhirter's Son would go down in history right alongside Mrs. O'Leary's Cow.

I did the usual things: lock up the matches, scold, threaten, cajole, explain, forbid, punish. No good. I don't know where he got them, but he did. One day I decided to yield something, let him win a point. I don't know why. Exhaustion, probably. Maybe it was Ed's idea.

This was back in the days when trash burning was *de rigueur*, and also legal. We usually did it, in the appropriate receptacle, once every week or 10 days. We told Jim he had been appointed the official family trash burner and he could burn trash once a day. (Kids aren't very good at deferred gratification.) There were stipulations, however: He had to get the garden hose out and handy, stoke the trash burner with bona fide trash and do his ritual burning nightly, after dinner and in the presence of Dad or Mom, as fire marshals. Yes, he could strike the matches, as many as it took or he wanted to use. Jim was ecstatic.

We had an official family trash burner for about two weeks. By then Jim was bored, and I figured he had lighted about seven pounds of book matches which must be the critical mass for a four-year-old. He asked to be relieved of his duties, and we agreed to his request.

The point of all of this is to say that we (that's the familial "we," the side of clout) won this case. James the Determined did not mess with matches after this contest of will. He accepted the judgment of the court. But we gave him his points. He was old enough to light matches, and he had a need to do so.

I think the same formula for winning, by giving away some points to the other guy, can be applied to man-woman conflicts, boss-employe disagreements and almost every adversary situation. It works.

— *April 17, 1978*

Do what's expected of you — and then do much more

No significant reward is ever realized from doing what other people expect of you.

That's our lesson for today. It's an immutable law of nature. Most people go to their graves without understanding it. Some people understand, but reject it. The world is full of fools.

The above is not to say one should ignore assigned responsibility or the expectations of others. Wrong. All responsibilities reasonably assigned and agreed to must be fulfilled cheerfully, fully and on time. You do it for your own self-respect, your own healthy ego.

If Mom says you are to clean your room on Saturday, then you clean your room on Saturday. Don't put the dirty clothes on the closet shelf either. And don't whine or grump that you'd rather be at the movies.

If the boss expects your report on the goober-gump deal on his desk first thing Tuesday morning, you work on it over the weekend and don't hit the sack Monday night until it's finished. Who cares if it's an unrealistic deadline? If Tuesday is what he wants, Tuesday is what you give him, with a smile.

If you are supposed to punch in at the Frisbee Plant at 7:30 a.m., you punch in at 7:30, not 7:37 or 7:48. I don't care if your bus was late. I don't care if your car broke down. Don't tell me your troubles, just be here when you are supposed to be here. Got that? There are lots of people who can use your job.

The reasonable expectations of others must be met. That's common sense.

The uncommon sense comes in knowing that you will receive no significant reward for meeting these expectations. Ha, if you thought you would, or think you should.

Mom will be pleased that you cleaned your room. That's all. She won't decide to increase your allowance or buy you the stereo of your dreams. She'll be pleased, and then she'll forget all about it, as she should.

Your boss will be glad to see the goober-gump report on his desk Tuesday morning. He's expecting it. Thanks. No applause. He may not even return your smile.

If you punch in at the Frisbee Plant at 7:30 a.m. for 40 years, never a minute late, that wins you not even the extra cookie in your boss' lunch box. Nobody will tell you you're a wonderful person. The best you'll get is no more chewing out because you're late.

Knowing this, the temptation is to cynicism. Small minds gravitate in that direction. Husbands who meet expectations and are not adored say their wives don't understand them. Wives who do all that is required of them and are not cherished say their husbands don't appreciate them. Everybody says life is a crock. It is reasonable and rewarding, if you don't try to fight natural law.

What do you want for your time and energy? You want praise, respect, love, money, fame, power and glory. You want significant reward.

Well, sir and ma'am, you can have it. But it doesn't come from meeting the expectations of others. That you will do that is taken for granted. What you get from meeting reasonable expectations is wages; you never get stock options and year-end bonuses. Persons who do what is expected are appreciated, but never lionized. Persons who do what is expected swell the parade, but never lead it.

Significant reward comes from doing more and better than expected. And you must set the goals. If you let someone else set higher goals for you than you have now, we get back to expectations again. You decide what you will achieve which will exceed all the expectations of those about you — in your family, your school, your office or work place. And I'd keep it secret. Just a little something between you and yourself.

You are now set to own the world.

Significant reward comes from overachievement. That doesn't mean superhuman work. It only means achieving more than was ever expected of you and doing so consistently, to the amazement of all.

This is a liberating idea. It is a power play. It's not difficult, and the only pressure comes from you, your own best friend. Sic 'em.

— Jan. 31, 1983

A run-of-the-mill mugging but a full-fledged trauma

A woman I know was mugged and had her purse stolen a few days ago. She's barely five feet tall and weighs as much as a gnat. She was a pushover, which is what her assailants did to her.

It was about 7 p.m., not yet anywhere near the dregs of night. The woman had stopped for groceries at a market in a small shopping center across from her downtown apartment building. As she left the store and walked through the parking area, four boys who looked like teenagers approached.

They knocked her around between them, grabbing for the purse. She screamed, dropped her groceries and shouted for help. None came.

The kids shoved the woman to her knees, dragged her along the ground briefly, tore loose the purse and ran off.

As the woman sat on the ground surrounded by her scattered groceries, a man walked to her side. He asked if she needed help. She did.

This good samaritan helped the woman collect her salvage and carried her groceries and walked her a few yards across the street to her apartment building. She was very grateful.

As muggings go, this one was mild. There was no lasting physical damage. The woman has some ugly bruises and scrapes but they'll heal. A good pair of wool slacks was shredded at the knees. A blouse is ready for the ragbag. The purse is gone, of course, along with about $85 cash, an assortment of credit cards and the usual clutter of personal treasures.

The lasting damage is psychological. The woman's hands still tremble days after this incident. Sleep is full of bad dreams. Tears are near the spillover level most of the time. They alternate with rage.

"Those little b-------," she says, without apology. "I feel so violated, so damaged." It was no rape, not even a serious physical assault. But she says she begins to understand the horror of being taken forcefully and abused, without humanity or compassion.

"But the very worst part," she says, "is that all the while I was being knocked around and I was calling for help, there were two grown men sitting in a car just a few feet away. They just watched. It was quite a show I know, but they didn't do a thing to help, not even yell at the kids. And there were other people coming and going from the stores. They just stood around and watched, too."

The man who eventually came to her aid had not seen the incident. He had been inside the grocery store.

Once she got home, the woman called the police. They came promptly and were polite, thorough in their questioning, and compassionate, she said. "But what can they do?" she wonders. Probably not much.

There are small comforts. The cash was mostly French francs, purchased because the woman plans a trip to Europe soon. The kids won't know what they are at first, what they're worth or how to convert them. That may take some of the fun out of it. The credit cards were reported stolen immediately. The woman's material losses are minimal. This was a small crime, just a practice run.

"I'll tell you something, though," says the victim. "I take back every nice thing I ever said about this neighborhood. I used to think it was safe and civilized and even enlightened. It's the pits. I hate it. I can't trust it or anybody in it, such as those men in that car. I'm moving, and just as soon as I can."

She won't move. She likes it where she is. It will take more than one mugging to get her to pack her bags. What she will do — has already done, in fact — is change her politics. It happened just that quickly, radically and perhaps irrationally.

— Oct. 17, 1983

Know what causes the Circa 30 Wobblies?

A painful malady strikes unmarried persons at about age 30. They get the wobblies. Two people I know are in the throes right now. Their friends are very concerned.

Much has been written about the agony of adolescence, which manifests itself earlier in zits and an inability to stand unless the legs are encased in Levis. Then there is the ever popular Mid-life Crisis, which comes along later and is instantly recognizable. Victims of M-lC file for divorce, change their hairstyles dramatically, start dating much younger partners and take disco dancing lessons.

I can't remember reading about the Circa 30 Wobblies in any of my scientific journals, however, including Psychology Today and People magazines. Obviously, there is a need for some basic research. I'll apply for the federal grant. Meanwhile, you can bone up on everything we know so far about the wobblies.

It afflicts both men and women although the symptoms vary slightly with sex. Women have more fits of depression. Men have anxiety syndrome. Both uncomfortable states of mind spring from the same cause: A sudden realization that the 30th birthday is approaching or has recently passed and no positive life-style change has occurred during the preceding five years. It's always five years. I don't know why.

"Look at me," you hear a female Wobblies victim moan. "It took my eyes until 11 o'clock to unpuff this morning. They've always made it by 10:15 before. I think it's bags. There are definitely little lines there. The chin could go any minute. And this job! Same crummy boss and the same crummy company. I never meet anybody new. I'll still be filing purchase orders when I've got bifocals and varicose veins. I'm still in the same apartment with that Salvation Army furniture I promised myself was only temporary. Same dumb boyfriends, same dumb parties. I've got to GET HOLD OF MY LIFE."

A male Wobblies sufferer says, "I think I made the wrong career choice. Why do I want to be a lawyer? I would rather be a plumber. No, a lawyer's OK, but I'm not making any money. I'll probably still be taking cheapo divorces when I'm 50. Maybe I should join a club, make some contacts. I can't afford to join a club. I should be doing SOMETHING, though; I'm THIRTY. I've got to GET HOLD OF MY LIFE."

What he and she usually do first is plan a vacation. She goes to Club Med and meets a shoe salesman from Cedar Rapids, Iowa. Boring. He goes to Las Vegas and meets an airline stewardess. Less boring but equally useless.

Next, these two plunge into self-betterment projects. He jogs and joins the "Y" to play handball or swim. She takes gourmet cooking lessons, buys a bicycle and joins an exercise class. Both take a series of solemn oaths: No more booze; no more junk food; lose weight; give up cigarets; get fit; find a hobby; get the wardrobe in order; paint the apartment; save money!

Sometimes people with the Wobblies actually do some or all of the above. It never helps much. The depression and anxiety are still there, just under the surface.

Almost never do Wobblies sufferers honestly address what ails them. Too scary.

The cruel, immutable truth is that they want to get married. Or, in the mildest cases, they can't shake the feeling that they SHOULD want to get married and they had better decide pretty fast if they're going to do it because time and opportunities are running out.

Women look in the mirror and recognize that they are not as moist and svelte as they were at 20 or 25. Marriageable males of appropriate age are fewer and fewer in number, and less and less interested in wrinkles and lumps they have not already learned to love.

Then, there are babies to consider. If a woman is to be a mother, she had better do it before she is 35, and even that's risky if you listen to the harpies around the water cooler. I know I want a career, but do I want to find myself 50 years old, living in an apartment with a cat? Will I have an occasional boyfriend who takes me bowling? Is that enough? Do I really want to pass on the idea of long-term love, marriage, children and grandchildren? These are some of the questions that give her the Wobblies.

He wonders how long he will be attractive to the boppers at the bars, and how long they will be attractive to him. Do I want to go from woman to woman to woman until I am 60 and find it necessary to buy them all clothes and trips and baubles in order to enjoy their company? Will I be lonesome and unhappy? Should I try to love somebody and hope she loves me back? What if she doesn't? What if she's a turkey? The divorce will clean me.

That's him doing the above thinking. Don't ask me for the answers: I have none. I am convinced, however, that the Circa 30 Wobblies arise from this root cause.

If sufferers can make it through to about age 35 without materially damaging their lives, the symptoms usually subside. Things settle down then for a few more years — until it's time for the Mid-life Crisis.

— Dec. 14, 1977

The middle muddle:
Is there no escape?

"I am a mediocre person," she says, smiling. "I have made it my life work and I think I am successful at it. Moderately successful, of course."

We are eating lunch and this long-time friend has chosen the place — a downtown bar and grill where we dine on hamburgers and pickles and Old Vienna draft. So-so. Appropriate. She continues her semiserious self-evaluation:

"Look at me," she says. "I'm not pretty, but I'm not ugly. I dress well, but I'm no fashion knockout. I took tennis and cooking and pottery-making lessons and I do all of those things in a mediocre way. I have a mediocre job for mediocre pay at a mediocre company in a mediocre town. There is absolutely nothing that I do really well, but there is nothing that I do really badly either."

"Are you happy?" I wonder. "Moderately, that is."

"Sort of," she says. "I have a mediocre boyfriend which helps, and we have a mediocre relationship."

I giggle and ask, "Were you ever extraordinary for any reason?"

"Well, when I was in kindergarten a teacher told my parents that I was an underachiever. That made me special. But Daddy asked her how much a five-year-old is expected to achieve in any given day and she backed off. Then, for a while, I was a certified overachiever, but I gave that up. Too much pressure. You don't get that kind of pressure when you are well established as mediocre. I settled on mediocrity as a life-style quite early."

Did we all? Probably, but I never thought about it before. In fact, achieving mediocrity in as many life facets as possible is apparently the American Dream. My friend and I discuss this and laugh at our discovery process.

We hope our children do well in school, but if they are super smart to super dull it will create problems for everybody.

We shop in supermarkets and shopping centers where there is nothing really rotten and nothing really swell.

We drive "moderately" priced cars that wear out in three years and don't really want the Rolls. Too worrisome.

We live in mediocre houses or apartments, designed by OK builders — never architects — and we furnish them with nylon carpet and Formica furniture — never Orientals and solid mahogany.

We stay in Holiday Inns and go to Disneyland. We eat those hamburgers and drink that draft beer. Or California wine. Or iced tea. Mediocre all the way.

"This is very depressing," I tell my friend. "Surely it's just a function of money. If we were wealthy, we would not be so mediocre."

"Wrong!" she says. "The rich are the most mediocre of all. That's why we all want to be like them."

How so?

"Well," she says, "Look at them. They go to Europe and Florida. Ever hear of one of them going to Peru? Never. They wear little black dresses and pearls. They drive Cadillacs. They live in Queen Anne chairs with crewel-embroidered upholstery. They never do anything spectacular or unusual or even unpredictable. Consistently mediocre."

Right!

"I think this is the only country in the world which encourages, idealizes and glorifies mediocrity," says she. "The Miss America contest should be a Miss Mediocre contest. Wait. I think it is. Of course it is!"

Right again. I ask my authority on mediocrity to name a mediocre glamor vacation. "Club Med," she says, without hesitation. How about a mediocre dinner out? "Surf and Turf, anyplace," she says, "with a baked potato and sour cream."

Dalton is a mediocre fashion label, says she; Vuitton is a mediocre status symbol.

"Is there no escape from this middle muddle?" I wonder. "I would like to have or be or do something that is better than mediocre."

"Whatever for?" asks my friend. "America isn't set up for it. You'll just get a headache trying."

"A headache sounds like a very mediocre ailment," say I.

"Naturally," says she.

I go home to try for a migraine.

— Aug. 12, 1977

Familiar, world-class lies are available to everybody

A couple of centuries ago I met a newspaperman who said, "Remember, everybody lies." I was shocked. I wrote my mentor off as a terminal cynic.

Experience, however, taught and continues to teach that he was correct and not necessarily cynical. Everybody lies, although not necessarily grossly or maliciously and not habitually.

What happens is just that, from time to time, everybody is sorely tempted to shave the truth just a little. Sometimes we are tempted to shave it a lot. Sometimes we are tempted to manufacture whole, huge and lavishly decorated untruths to use as substitutes for reality.

I have made a modest study of lies.

The ones which intrigue me most are not the laser-like lies employed to some specific, unique purpose. You have to be there and be personally involved to appreciate those things. The lies that fascinate me are the archetypes, in the public experience and domain.

I have been trying to put together a list of all-time world-class lies. These are versatile, general purpose lies — the ones we recognize for what they are, but still can't refute.

"I am not a crook!" does not qualify. It's a pretty good lie (Whopper division, Plain type) which everyone recognizes, but it lacks greatness because so few of us have any opportunity to use it. Besides, it has no style.

"I did not eat the piece of pie you were saving for Joey. A giant bug crawled out of Joey's baseball glove, squirted me with poison gas, and, when I woke up, I had crumbs on my chin and the pie was gone. Honest, Mom!" This is a very stylish little lie (Trifle division, Fancy type) but much too incident-specific for the rest of us to utilize.

World-class lies all have a certain universality, plus arrogance or hauteur. And they are unchallengeable, even when we know they are untrue statements.

The lie which tops my world-class list, so far, embodies the essence of championship lying. You'll recognize it immediately. It is:

"I couldn't lie to you."

This is a lot like "I wouldn't lie to you," but it is a cut above. The liar flatters by saying "couldn't." It is as if the person being lied to is so wise that no liar would have a chance. How can anyone argue with that?

Another world-class lie is the fabled, "The check is in the mail." It leaves the adversary standing on one foot, sucking his or her thumb.

"I welcome a second opinion" is definitely world-class. Its hauteur is majestic.

Others on my world-class list include, "I don't mean to pry, but . . ." and "I'm really surprised that you're so upset about this."

There is a whole-group of world-class lies that have evolved from the love-marriage-divorce equation. This could be the mother lode. Entries include:

"My wife (husband) doesn't understand me."

"I promise no one will ever know about this, except us."

"I know you're disappointed, but I promise to make it up to you."

"I can't believe you're jealous!"

"I only stay married for the sake of the children."

"This is the first time I've ever cheated on my wife (husband)."

"That was the last time I'll ever cheat on you, Sweetheart."

"I'll call you tomorrow, for sure, count on it."

"I want to be with you, too, but the boss insists I stay here and finish this project even if it takes all night (week, month)."

"The reason there wasn't any answer when you called last night is because my phone was out of order."

"Me? Having an affair? The whole idea is just too ridiculous to discuss."

"I love you much too much to let you get hooked on me; I'm no good; you deserve better."

World-class lies, every one — tough, durable, utilitarian and blatantly false, but impregnable. Remember them.

— *Aug. 13, 1981*

If you are THE greatest, try a little underwhelming

The topic today is underwhelming. This is a kind of courtship technique especially recommended for older males, newly liberated females, all persons who have graduated from assertiveness training classes and smart-mouthed female columnists. Some such persons tend to give the impression that they know it all. They can't understand why everybody else doesn't applaud them for that. There are reasons.

Just because you have learned to ask for what you want, can say "yes" and "no" without apology or guilt and figure you have most of the answers to civilization's sticky questions is no reason to expect fan clubs to pop up all over the western world. Not everybody has your advantages. Just because you are able to look at yourself in the mirror and see a Prince rather than a frog does not suggest that you should gallop about the kingdom posting royal proclamations of your own wonderfulness either. Tacky.

At a party recently I was approached by a man who swooped across the room like a giant condor. He perched at my side, smiling. After the "Hello, my name is ... " the condor attempted to transport me to some mountaintop of ecstasy by telling me he was powerful, bright, charming and bursting with eagerness to share some of this with some lucky woman, perhaps myself. So he said.

He scared the bejeepers out of me. I tap-danced out of range.

"What's wrong with that guy?" I asked a friend at this do. "I dunno," was the answer. "I guess he is proud of himself and figures you would be honored by his attention if you knew. So he told you."

"It was a definite turnoff," said I eloquently, choking on a grape.

"It was no brag," said the friend. "All that stuff is true."

"It's a turnoff because he overwhelmed me!" I whined. "He made me feel what? Diminished? Inadequate maybe. A little silly for sure. Over my head!" And that's the truth.

It isn't easy to warm up to somebody who towers over you like an Alp any more than it is easy to adore someone who scuttles around your ankles. I have a feeling that friendships or whatever (especially whatever) are possible only when the parties perceive themselves as equals, more or less. They may not be equals in their work or by most or any measures, but they have to establish equality on the emotional playfield somehow or there isn't going to be any game.

A knowledge of underwhelming techniques is essential then for all highly assertive and overachieving persons, for persons of wealth and power or for others who are just natural born wowsers. (Robert Redford comes to mind.)

The essence of underwhelming is exposing vulnerability. Not everything, for heaven's sake. Nobody wants to hear you whine or tell all about your nightmares or ugly habits. We just need to know you are human and not plastic perfection. It isn't hard.

We all have weaknesses which we try to hide or ignore. A dragon with a fondness for jelly beans is kind of cute, however. That's how vulnerability can work for dragons. Without the jelly beans, forget it.

I wonder how we overlooked this. Kid literature is full of the lovableness of weak or flawed creatures. The Ugly Duckling is the adored one. Pinocchio has a great deal of trouble with his lies and overgrown nose. There is poor, pitiful Beast, ultimately loved by sweet Beauty. Dorothy the confused with her Cowardly Lion, Tin Woodman and Scarecrow are certainly imperfect critters. And Jack, of beanstalk fame, would never get our cheers for offing the Giant if he weren't terrified all the while he's at it.

It is not just because these things were written for kids that the heroes are vulnerable. The tradition continues into adult literature and certainly into the theater and the movies.

Hamlet and Othello have their weak, soft, underbellies. In Othello's case it is a hard head, but it works the same way. And who could not love Gary Cooper or Jimmy Stewart eversomuch more than whoever played the invincible, implacable villain? The shuffling, scratching, suffering and indecision were endearing.

We like our heroes slightly flawed and definitely vulnerable. Otherwise we cannot love them or empathize. We are all vulnerable; that's why. And we know it.

So, in this matter of courting and carrying on, there is no reason to waste time on obvious success and perfection. It is highly recommended that the strong among us display a little weakness.

It is appropriate, for example, to admit confusion or indecision on some subject. You can invite opinions and listen without argument. It is reassuring to common folk to think uncommon folk don't have all the answers.

You can admit having tried and failed at something. That is usually well accepted. No excuses based on acts of others or God or the economy are allowed. And the whole exercise is nullified once you say, "Of course, it didn't really matter." It is absolutely despicable to imply that you somehow profited by your failure. A pox upon those who say, "Seemed a disaster at the time but, you know, I eventually made $40 million from that episode. Eh, eh, eh." Eh, eh, YECH! If you're going to fail, damn it, FAIL.

Another possible is confessing that from time to time you succumb to a compulsion to do something simple and definitely unchic. Pigging out on peanut butter sandwiches would do, for example, or riding a bike. Just a beat-up bike, however; tell us no tales of Lamborghini 20-speeds with Ghia styled sheet metal and saddles by Gucci. And, if you ever won a bicycle race, I don't want to hear about it.

Underwhelming demands this display of vulnerability coupled with honesty and good humor. It is the equalizer. It banishes fear and awe and makes all people not exactly just plain folks but, at least, emotionally accessible to each other.

After explaining all of this, the oracle McWhirter is going back to Delphi to counsel with the gods. She, of course, is ever perfect and never errs.

— April 25, 1980

Each of us is unique and irrevocably alone

Each of us is unique, singular, in the universe. We all know it, but most of the time the concept hunches there in a dusty corner of our brain and we are functionally oblivious to it. That's probably just as well because when it jumps up, and we remember, it can be terrifying.

I saw a bumper sticker recently which said, "Be the Best Possible You." It gave me the shivers. It's supposed to be uplifting and ego-gratifying to remember you are one of a kind and inimitable. Maybe it can be if you are very brave, very strong and the General Chaos has slipped you a blueprint and spec sheet with your name on it. Otherwise, shivers.

"How do I do it? What is it?" I shout at the smug Whozit driving the car. "Give me one clue!" If ever I rack up on the freeway it will be because of some Whozit with an outrageous bumper sticker.

Being unique implies certain corollaries which are definitely unsettling.

COROLLARY I: Each of us is irrevocably alone.

Sure, we may have friends galore and relatives a-go-go, but no two of us are even similar. Identical twins, like cloned frogs, are biological duplicates. But anybody who has spent much time around twins knows they do not think, respond or feel identically, or even similarly, much of the time. Twinning is as close as human beings ever come to meeting themselves coming and going. We can forget about finding anyone much like ourselves and certainly no duplicates. No role models exist, not even perfect heart, mind and soul mate.

Love doesn't unify. Lovers, married or otherwise, are as separate and distinct as two orchids growing under separate bell jars on the same window sill. I'm not sure orchids grow on window sills, but that doesn't matter.

A woman once told me how she felt making love to her husband. These two were much in love and recently married, so I figured this was as good as it got. "I can't get close enough," she said. "I want every cell of my body to merge with every cell of his so that we become one person, one flesh, just as we promised in our wedding vows. No way. The closer we are physically, the more I am aware of how separate we are. I would like to experience his sensations and thoughts from the inside and have him know mine the same way. We can't do it. We talk about how good it would be."

It's a cheat, for sure. Every body cell has a wall and every clump of cells has a wall and every whole, entire body has a wall and every person is a prisoner in solitary confinement within a multi-walled fortress. We look out through stained glass windows at each other's moving, legged prisons.

We haven't even been very successful in our attempts to communicate between prisons. We invented spoken languages and body languages and some of us have experimented with psychic languages. We are inventive. All of it, especially the latter, is unreliable and imprecise. Pitiful.

COROLLARY II: Communication between isolated persons in the universe is extremely difficult, takes great effort and is subject to gross misinterpretation.

So, here we are, each of us unlike any other and unable to experience the essence of any other and unable to communicate with any other accurately or dependably. Some of us don't even try. Like Ray Bradbury space cadets, we are individually encapsulated and caroming through the universe, listening to garble and static on jammed up radios.

"Be the Best Possible You" — no wonder it gives me the shivers. I have no way of knowing what that is, or if I am even headed in the right direction. I am unique. So are you. Being unique and solitary in the universe is not something particularly ego-gratifying. It is a frightening experience, which is probably why we invented holding hands in the movies.

— April 3, 1978